$10.00

THE MINISTRY OF

MUSIC
IN THE
BLACK
CHURCH

J. WENDELL MAPSON, JR.

Judson Press ® Valley Forge

To my parents,

Rev. and Mrs. J. Wendell Mapson, Sr.,

who, when I was very young,

told me about Christ

THE MINISTRY OF MUSIC IN THE BLACK CHURCH

Copyright © 1984
Judson Press, Valley Forge, PA 19482-0851

Unless otherwise indicated, Bible quotations in this volume are from the
Revised Standard Version of the Bible copyrighted 1946, 1952 © 1971, 1973
by the Division of Christian Education of the National Council of the Churches
of Christ in the U.S.A., and used by permission.

Other quotations of the Bible are from the HOLY BIBLE New International
Version, copyright © 1978, New York International Bible Society. Used by
permission.

Library of Congress Cataloging in Publication Data

Mapson, J. Wendell.
  The ministry of music in the black church.

  Bibliography:
  1. Church music—Instruction and study. 2. Afro-Americans—Music. I.
Title.
MT88.M17 1984   783'.02'608996073   84-12246
ISBN 0-8170-1057-2

95 96 97 98 99 00 01 02   13 12 11 10 9 8 7 6

Acknowledgments

I am deeply indebted to Eastern Baptist Theological Seminary, Philadelphia, Pennsylvania, for the opportunity, through my involvement in the Doctor of Ministry program, to be challenged on a deeper level of what it means to minister.

I am also indebted to Dr. William D. Thompson, professor of preaching at the seminary and chairman of my thesis-project committee, for his guidance and direction throughout the duration of this project; Dr. Wendell Phillips Whalum, professor of music at Morehouse College, Atlanta, Georgia, who served as a member of the committee and who offered valuable suggestions and insight along the way; Dr. Myron Chartier, director of doctoral programs at the seminary, in whose classes my understanding of ministry was expanded; and Dr. Wallace C. Smith, assistant professor of pastoral theology and ministry at the seminary, whose involvement in the black experience proved beneficial in my quest to be faithful to the Afro-American tradition.

My thanks go to my typist, Ms. Juanita Corum, who read the manuscript and whose typing skills were invaluable.

I will always be grateful to the Union Baptist Church for giving me the freedom to reenter the arena of academic pursuit so that for them I might become a better steward of what God has entrusted to those of us who minister.

My thanks go also to one of the organists of the Union Baptist Church, Belinda D. Scott, who has cooperated with me and helped lift the music ministry in our own church.

CONTENTS

Preface

I have been in the black church and have lived in a parsonage all of my life, the results of being the son of a black Baptist minister. I was born in the South, and though I was raised in the North, the "southern stamp," along with its cultural influences, is yet upon me and shall remain so.

My parents saw to it that all of their children were exposed to piano lessons at early ages. As a result, my love for music runs deep, especially for the music of the black religious experience. In my formative years, after much parental prodding, I became pianist for the Sunday church school in my father's church and, later, organist for the junior choir. During my days at Morehouse College in Atlanta, Georgia, I was organist for various area churches.

Through the years I have remained sensitive to the music of the black church but not to the point of rubber-stamping all that comes forth as an authentic religious expression. I have seen instances when worship seemed to degenerate into something less than what God intended, and I wondered if, in fact, God's Spirit was present in those situations. I have been in worship services in which the music became a hindrance to divine-human dialogue. I have talked to black pastors, many of them well trained academically, who shared my concerns but who seemed hesitant to explore "foreign soil" without compass. I began to see the need for a more critical examination of the components of the music of the black religious experience.

The opportunity for such an undertaking availed itself while I was a student at the Eastern Baptist Theological Seminary. Thus I chose a thesis project for a Doctor of Ministry degree that would allow me to address this important area of pastoral ministry from the black perspective. Some of the material in the original study has been omitted or, in a few instances, rearranged for this book.

The purpose, then, of this book is to provide guidelines for the qualitative use of music in the black church. These guidelines are included in chapters 1 through 7. Chapter 8 is an attempt to appraise what I have done in light of the evaluations of others who are competent in the field. I do not pretend to be a professional musician, and I do not write from such a perspective. However, as writer, I approach the subject with considerable music appreciation and training, and I intend to raise issues of pastoral leadership and concern in the context of church music and worship.

Because music is such a vital component in the worship experience of the black church, it is important that we seek to understand its relationship to theology and that we set out to become more faithful and worthy stewards of the gifts God has entrusted to our care.

CHAPTER ONE

Music
in the Black Tradition

Music has always been a necessary thread in the fabric out of which the human spirit was created. From ancient times to the present day, music has filled in the gaps made by humanity's attempt to express the inexpressible. As Debussy observed, music "reaches the naked flesh of feeling."

This is especially true when considering the religious pilgrimage of the human race. Worship forms and practices have been designed to assist in humankind's quest to find meaning and purpose. And music has been part and parcel of deity worship from the dawn of civilization.

The Judeo-Christian heritage attests to the importance of musical expression. It would be impossible to imagine the people of God without a song. Evidence is plentiful that music played an important role in the Hebrew worship of Yahweh. The psalms attest to the importance of music in the worship of God.

Even though the New Testament church was composed of a variety of forms and practices, all of these expressions sprang from Jewish roots. The New Testament church was a reflection of Jewish forms. Even though the evidence is not as pronounced, we know that the early Christian church emphasized music as an integral part of worship and praise to God. In the early church, music belonged to the congregation, and Scripture makes many references to the practice of singing. Some of the most beautiful passages in the New Testament are ancient hymns, borrowed and recast by the biblical writers to fit a particular theological purpose.

Toward a Better Way

The tasks of ministers and musicians are to monitor and examine the music of the church, specifically the music of the black worship experience, and to see whether or not the people of God are giving their best. Traditions must be constantly reexamined. An attempt should be made, not only to reflect the best of the Afro-American tradition, but also to be true to the biblical model.

One of the purposes of this book, then, is to make contemporary black ministers more aware of the issues with which they must deal if they are serious about correcting the abuses within the church that relate to music and worship. Such correction is an educational task. To accomplish this task, the reader must glean some understanding of the nature and meaning of music as reflected in the history of Israel and in the churches of the New Testament. The people of God have always been a singing people, and their experiences have always given shape to their song.

Another purpose of this book is to take a closer look at the pastor-musician-choir-congregation relationship. Even though singing is not an end in itself, neither is it a means of filling in the gaps in the worship experience. Music is not to act as a piece of scenic background. Songs should not be sung just because they are on the "top ten" gospel list. The congregation is not ever to be spectator but, through a strange spiritual encounter, is to become participant. The function of the choir is to worship as well as to sing. This book will take a deeper look at this complex set of relationships in order to aid the examination of the issues to be raised.

Still another aim of this book is to take a look at how the state of music in the black church has developed. Usually cultural trends take place over a period of time and cannot be traced to any one cause. In studying the development of these cultural trends, my intention is not to remove from black culture that which has given power, substance, and life to black religion but to preserve the best of the black faith heritage and to foster continual growth and creativity out of which its music was and continues to be born. One must not only speak of the past relevance of the black church but must also address the question of continuing relevance. The genius of the black slaves was in their ability to apply a "contemporary hermeneutic" to the situation in which they found themselves. They did, in effect, "sing the Lord's song in a strange land" (Psalm 137:4). To a large extent the land is still strange. But a song must be sung.

A Black Point of View

When speaking of black religion, it may be an understatement to say that music has always been a necessary ingredient in the religion of the Afro-American. In this case, music has been more than a mere ingredient. It has been the yeast that has given shape, substance, and content to the black religious experience.

First of all, when one stops speaking of religion and begins speaking of black religion, that person immediately risks compartmentalizing the whole of religious experience. However, it must be recognized that societies already are imposed with labels that have, to a large extent, defined the parameters of human existence. The people of various societies filter their behavior, view of reality, religious beliefs, and identity through different cultural screens.

Inevitably the question must be asked, "What is black religion?"

Henry Mitchell names some characteristics of black religion.[1] First, he finds a uniqueness of black culture in the freedom of expression observed in the pulpit and the congregation of any given church. A second, closely related characteristic in the black worship experience is what he calls "ritual freedom," that is, the spirit dictates, and not the printed order of worship, who shall participate, when, and for how long. Akin to this second characteristic is the freedom found in the music of black worship. The black church has "melodic license" and makes uninhibited use of improvisation.

African Roots and Influence

Even though much has been written in recent years about African roots, it may be well to identify some of the characteristics in order to say how the past has shaped the present state of affairs in the black church.

Miles Mark Fisher, in his book *Negro Slave Songs in the United States*, identifies some of the characteristics of African culture, especially as they relate to the music and worship practices of the African. It might first be noted that religion, as well as music, was deeply embedded in the whole of African life. African thought was not compartmentalized and fragmented. The African's view of the world was holistic. Even the distinction in Western culture between "sacred" and "secular" did not apply in African culture. Music was part of every event and experience in the life of the African society. Music told the unwritten story of the history of a given community.

Eileen Southern describes the style of singing in African culture. "The singing style employed by the Africans was characterized by high intensity and use of such special effects as falsetto, shouting, and guttural tones."[2] In terms of musical form:

The most constant feature of African songs was the alternation of improvised lines and fixed refrains. This form allowed for both innovative and conservative procedures at the same time: the extemporization of verses to suit the specific occasion and the retention of traditional words in the refrains; the participation of the soloist in the verses and of the group in singing the refrains; improvisation or embellishment upon the solo melody and reinforcement of the traditional tune in the refrains.[3]

Dena Epstein seeks to trace African roots and contends that one must look in such places as Jamaica and the West Indies for additional sources. She says that West Indian accounts give valuable information about the music of slaves that could not be gathered in mainland reports. She concludes that "African musics were transplanted to the New World by the second half of the seventeenth century." Musical instruments in use at the time included drums, rhythm sticks, banjos, musical bows, quills or panpipes, and a form of xylophone called the balafo.[4]

African Influence in the New World

The arrival of a few African slaves at Jamestown in 1619 was the beginning of another chapter in the history of the New World. The scars of slavery have already been well documented. The important point to remember is that the African slaves brought with them components of a culture which could not and would not be extinguished in the new land. This was due, in part, to the persistence of an oral tradition. Knowing this tradition is vital to understanding the continuation of musical forms and practices *during* slavery. (Note that slavery did not destroy these forms and practices.)

Even though slaves in the New World were separated from family and kin and from those of common tongue, the musical forms of African culture were retained. Wyatt Tee Walker notes that with no common tongue, the musical expression was reduced to chants and moans on the rhythm forms and in the musical idioms that survived. As the slaves learned the language of the masters, their verbal commonality became most pronounced in the music that developed in the context of slavery.[5]

The emergence of what E. Franklin Frazier calls the "invisible church" was a logical consequence of the desire of the slaves to maintain continuity with the past, and the form of worship in the "secret meetings" was akin to the forms of worship in the motherland. In these services, the tone was altogether different from the tone of the plantation owners' services.

One of the characteristics of this tone can be identified as "call and response." Southern notes:

> Modern scholars often use the term "call and response" to describe the responsorial or antiphonal nature of African song performance—i.e. the alternation of solo passages and choral refrains or of two different choral passages. Typically, a song consisted of the continuous repetition of a single melody, sung alternately by the song leader and the group, or alternately by two groups. The importance of the song leader cannot be overstressed: it was he who chose the song to be sung, who embellished the basic melody and improvised appropriate verses to fit the occasion, and who brought the performance to an end.[6]

Another feature of the music of the slaves was its improvisational quality. A genius of the slaves was their ability to create new songs from old melodies and to improvise upon various themes. Those who heard the slave melodies found it quite difficult to explain or define what they heard.

In order to understand the culture of black people, one must study African culture. In research done by Miles Mark Fisher, he suggests that music was the means by which the African people commented on their laws, customs, and history. "Folk historians" in every town were "living" encyclopedias. In various life situations there was music: on the battlefield, in secret meetings, at marriages and funerals, at child birth, in hunting, and in recreation.

Fisher concludes that five statements can be postulated concerning the importance of spirituals as historical documents. First, "the primary function of African music was to give the history of a people." Second, "African Negroes were transplanted to the Americas along with their gifts of song." Third, "the first extended collection of slave songs was advertised as historical documents from the Negro people." Fourth, "such an evolution of slave songs was perceived by divers people." And, fifth, "Negro spirituals are best understood in harmony with this historical interpretation."[7]

To deny that there are identifiable characteristics of black culture and religion and, therefore, music is to deny that any culture has an identity of its own. No matter how cultures may overlap and the degree to which they are assimilated, each culture has identifiable characteristics. It is also denying the existence of various forms of witness within the "churches" of the New Testament. To affirm the expression of faith as given to those of Afro-American descent is to recognize the extent to which cultures have responded to the activity of God in the world.

Black Theology and Black Music

Black theology deals with how black people see God, the world, and themselves from the vantage point of the oppressed.

> "I have indeed seen the misery of my people in Egypt. I have heard them crying out because of their slave drivers, and I am concerned about their suffering. I have come down to rescue them . . ." (Exodus 3:7, 8).

Black religion is a response to God's initiative, articulated through the thought forms, music, art, and customs of African culture. Black music comments on the history of that pilgrimage; a journey of sorrow, joy, despair, hope, frustration, and fulfillment.

The task, then, is to affirm the good in black theology and to offer correctives so that black theology may continue to address the needs of black people in light of their relationship to God and culture.

Historically, as has been shown, music in the black church has reflected the theology of the pilgrimage of black people. Set within the context of the black church, the religious music of black people has helped to articulate the very soul and substance of the black experience, most especially for those who belong to the family of God.

In many instances, music has not only been shaped by theology but has also shaped theology. Not only may one speak of a theology of music, but one might also speak of the music of theology. There is no doubt that in the black church music is the lifeblood. Among blacks, music is not always compartmentalized into categories such as sacred and secular. In fact, the black church itself does not always see itself in light of such labels. Among Afro-Americans, just as in African culture, religion permeates the whole of life, and so does music.

Here a distinction must be made between the folk religion of the black masses and the religion of those blacks who are part of a more institutionalized form of religion and have been influenced to a greater extent by white culture. It would appear that musical expression is much more significant among blacks who make up the middle- to lower-class structures.

Henry Mitchell also speaks of the "call and response" element in black preaching.[8] To a large extent the power of the sermon is determined by how well the black preacher can "sing" the sermon. Such matters as voice intonation, style, and sermonic rhythm help determine the success and popularity of many black preachers. Especially is this true among blacks who have made no attempt to "whiten" their culture.

This is not to suggest that black congregations do not value preparation, both academic and spiritual, and the content of the sermon. The black preacher must preach to the needs of the people. The preaching style only highlights the extent to which music is embedded in the entire worship experience of the black church.

To a large extent, a black church is judged by its spiritual tone, most often reflected in its ministry of music and worship. Often music is the vehicle by which the masses of black people are initially drawn into the community of faith. Many people join a particular church because that church has a "good" choir. Of course, that does not mean that such people attracted to a church because of the music are necessarily serious about the church's real ministry, which runs far deeper than superficial attractions.

Evidence of Erosion

Increasingly, music in the black church has been separated from its theological and historical underpinnings. Instead of serving theology as a legitimate response to God and telling the story of hardship, disappointment, and hope, music in the black church has become, in many instances, an end in itself. This often fosters the goal of entertainment rather than the goal of ushering people into the very presence of the Almighty and sending them forth to serve.

J. Deotis Roberts offers a valuable insight into the proper understanding of the relationship between black theology and music. He says,

> Our theological task is to supply a theological underpinning for meaning in black life. Black churches are now experiencing a great influx of black youth because of the popularity of gospel music. . . . But the underlying reason for the enchantment with the "gospel sound" may be a profound search for purpose and value in life. Gospel music is emotional and otherworldly. It has little if anything to do with

finding meaning for life in a hostile world. Unless we are able to anchor the celebration in Biblical faith and personal and social ethics, our success story will have a short history.[9]

More and more, music in the black church has become commercialized and packaged. Some of its lyrics represent poor theology, which has no place in black churches seeking to present the best of the faith heritage. As a result, the black church runs the risk of misusing this vital and necessary component of the faith.

Two of the responsibilities of the black church are to preserve its rich musical heritage as well as to create new music. One of the forms of this heritage is called the Negro spiritual. In many instances the spirituals, or "stories in music," have been abandoned, and generations of black boys and girls are growing up with no appreciation for black history as recorded in the spirituals. These "social commentaries" are yet relevant, for they speak today in a society in which despair and hope punctuate the human spirit.

The music of the black religious experience was born out of struggle and represents genuine emotion and motivation. In many instances what exists today is an attempt to copy what has already been packaged and to bury the gift of the creative spirit behind electronic instruments and assembly-line lyrics.

The singing of hymns has always been a great experience in the black worship idiom, and often hymns sound differently when sung in black churches than when they are sung in white churches. Frequently these hymns have been just about removed from the order of worship. Many choirs who sing gospel music loud and clear can hardly be heard when the time comes to sing a congregational hymn. Even when hymns are sung, they have been "gospelized" to the point at which their true beauty cannot be appreciated.

Another evidence of decay is the less frequent use of the old meter hymns, born in England, brought to New

England, and adopted by blacks. They are a solid fixture in the black religious heritage, and the preservation of the meter-hymn style of singing should be ensured by our learning them from a dying breed of southern blacks and teaching them to our young.

The Abuse of the Black Heritage

Obviously, the social context of blacks has helped to shape and define their institutions. Systematically barred from full participation in the large society, blacks have had to develop support systems of their own creation. The black church has not only served a religious function but has been an all-purpose institution, providing social as well as spiritual services. Much like the synagogue of Judaism, the black church has been the center of black life. From it came self-help organizations, resources for extended families, educational opportunities, and political organization. It provided a place for the free display of talent and potential that could not be utilized and appreciated in America's marketplace. Those who were powerless had access to power within the black church. Those who had neither title nor position elsewhere could hold office in the black church. Those who could not release their feelings in the everyday world could be heard on Sunday morning. The black church was and is both a place of temporary withdrawal as well as a place to refuel for the journey.

Even though the sharp distinction between "sacred" and "secular" does not exactly fit the black experience in religion, it can be postulated that the rise of secularism in the larger society has had an effect upon the secularization of music within the black church. When gospel music came into prominence in the 1930s and was popularized by the recording industry in the 1940s, many blacks initially resisted this "honky-tonk" music, as it was called. Even though the advent of pianos and organs was initially seen as profane, the present movement toward drums, guitars, and tamborines has been seen by some as a further contamination of a rich and glorious heritage. During the latter part of this century, the rhythm of the spirituals and meter hymns has been replaced by the beat of the gospel song.

Of course it is not the use but the abuse of this music form that causes such concern. This is not to suggest that other forms cannot or have not been subject to abuse and misuse. It is to suggest, however, that the music prevalent in many black churches today more easily lends itself to the possibility of abuse, if the direction it is taking is allowed to persist unchecked. The worship experience demands discipline as well as freedom, which is a constant theme of the apostle Paul. To paraphrase Cullmann, Paul sought to balance the "free expression of the Holy Spirit" with the "binding character of liturgy."

It is necessary to continue to affirm the power and appeal of music in the black church. Just as the Africans were a musical people, so Afro-Americans are a musical people. In the black church the two major attractions are still good preaching and good singing, although perhaps not always in that order. Already I have alluded to the way in which the preaching of the gospel is punctuated with musical intonations. The power of worship is in the music, and music's importance must continue to be affirmed. Blacks seem to tolerate poor preaching if the services can be redeemed by good singing.

It must also be recognized that the masses of black people have been attracted to the churches through gospel music rather than hymns. However, it is still necessary to guard against the temptation to give people what we think they want without critical examination of what is offered and of what they need.

Pastoral Leadership

In the black church the pastors have a great deal of freedom to shape, define, and influence the worship experience. More than any other persons, pastors are expected to lead in worship. Their responsibilities include encouraging and insisting that the congregation give its best to God and overseeing the entire ministry of the church. Even though the pastors of black congregations may not be musicians, they must be in touch with the issues relevant to the quality of music that comes forth from the worshiping congregation. Unfortunately, the seminary does not always equip pastors in the development of a theology of church music.

One of the problems is that ministers often take a hands-off policy rather than be intentional as they engage in ministerial transactions within the church. The minister has the responsibility and challenge to define, interpret, and plan those areas that will absorb the resources and energies of the congregation.

Toward a Theology of Music and Worship in the Black Idiom

What, then, is black worship? It is the corporate reflection by black people upon the acts of God as he responds to the theological, sociocultural, and political needs of black people. A theology of worship must, then, reflect the cultural peculiarities of blacks and, at the same time, rest upon the biblical foundations that have historically shaped the direction and destiny of Afro-Americans.

What, then, are some of the characteristics of black worship at its best? To ask further, how can one, in fact, test the following guidelines against the biblical and cultural norm? How does one determine whether the music that enters worship represents the best of the Afro-American heritage?

First, music in the black church must express the communal nature of the black experience. This does not mean that music expressing the desires of the individual should be rejected. It does mean, however, that the individual finds meaning through identity with cosufferers, with those who walk the same existential path.

James Cone expresses the individual-within-community concept when he says, "Black music is unifying because it confronts the individual with the truth of black existence and affirms that black being is possible only in a communal context."[10]

Cone's understanding is in line with the biblical norm and the apostle Paul's concept of the building up of the family of God (1 Corinthians 14:3-4; Ephesians 4:12). In the Corinthian passage, Paul tested the value of the diversity of gifts against his norm of edification. He said, "He who speaks in a tongue edifies himself, but he who prophesies edifies the church." (Although New Testament scholars debate the Pauline authorship of Ephesians, Pauline theology in Ephesians is evident.) Music in the black church must edify the family of God as it places the individual within the context of the community.

Second, music in the black church must hold in tension the emphasis on this world and the expectations of the new age. It must be "this worldly" without being materialistic and earthbound. It must be "other worldly" without being disconnected from the concerns of social justice. Music is to minister to the whole person. This is the task of black churches seeking to be true to their heritage. Some churches are not seeking to be true to their heritage.

Third, music in the black church must balance the freedom of the Holy Spirit with liturgical restriction. Spontaneity must be tempered with a sense of order and meaningful content. Emotion in black worship must be affirmed, but emotionalism must be discouraged.

Fourth, the black church must continue to be a place for celebration, and such celebration must continually be reflected in the music. Blacks have always gathered for worship expecting celebration to happen.

No doubt music will always be a vital component of the religious pilgrimage of black Americans. As it has done in the past, music must continue to comment on the hopes, fears, disappointments, and faith of a people who still must struggle to "sing the Lord's song in a strange land." Just as the early Christians initially gathered each Lord's day to celebrate the resurrection, so blacks will continue each Sunday morning to share in that victory over the unjust social structures that still need to be dismantled, so that "The kingdom of the world has become the kingdom of our Lord and of his Christ; and he shall reign for ever and ever" (Revelation 11:15).

CHAPTER TWO

A Biblical
Understanding of Worship

The church, as well as other institutions, does not exist in a vacuum but is part of a heritage and a tradition that reaches back through the centuries. Whatever the contemporary cultural leanings may be, Christians are linked together by the biblical witness. Each believer who is a part of the church of Jesus Christ belongs to a larger network of tradition and practices that has influenced his or her own religious contexts and provided foundations upon which the entire Christian community shall build.

Whether it is true or not, Christians like to think they are faithful heirs of that biblical faith and that their policies and practices and theology have scriptural legitimacy or, at least, bear a strong resemblance to the biblical faith. The purpose of this chapter is to survey the biblical record and draw some guidelines by which the current trends of music and worship in the black church can be tested. Let us begin with Israelite worship. How might we understand it?

The Nature of Israelite Worship

First, Israel's worship was God-centered. It was human response to divine initiative. It could be argued that Israel had no worship and, therefore, no song until God acted in a historical moment and set forth a plan of redemption to Moses at the burning bush.

> Then the LORD said, "I have seen the affliction of my people who are in Egypt, and have heard their cry because of their taskmasters; I know their sufferings, and I have come down to deliver them out of the hand of the Egyptians, and to bring them up out of that land to a good and broad land, a land flowing with milk and honey . . ." (Exodus 3:7-8).

Worship, then, was a natural and necessary consequence of God's redeeming activity in Israel's history.

Second, the worship of Israel was influenced by Israel's monotheistic faith, proclaimed time and time again through festivals and feasts and in the Shema. In the experience of Israelite worship this proclamation was given shape, form, and song.

Third, music was a natural expression of the Israelites' faith and was meaningful only within the context of worship. Music became a natural handmaiden of Israel's theology. This fusion of worship, music, and theology can be seen from the beginning of Israel's history.

Fourth, there was a surprising degree of spontaneity and freedom in the Israelite practice of worship and in the compilation and selection of Israel's music. The psalms themselves were not arranged in any logical sequence. It is interesting that the most important "songbook" of the Hebrew people has no identifiable literary structure. Even the divisions of Psalms into five sections may have been done to correspond with the five books of the Law.

In spite of the ritualism and legalism associated with the Jews of the Old Testament, there was a striking spontaneity evident in the selection of Scripture and psalms used in worship. In synagogue worship, the "ruler" would summon the "minister" to invite someone from the congregation to lead in the Shema, as it was recited antiphonally, or to read the Scripture. Perhaps this was how Jesus was called upon to read from the prophet Isaiah when he went into the synagogue at the beginning of his ministry (Luke 4:16-20).

Fifth, there was no contradiction between the worship aspect of Israel's life and the prophetic denouncements that seem to target the practice of worship. These two strands of Israel's tradition are not antithetical. It must be remembered that those prophets who denounced worship and, along with it, music were addressing themselves to the ills and decay of the whole nation. They were condemning worship that had become poisoned with the nation's malady. The prophets knew that the health of the nation was reflected in worship practices. They saw the misuses of worship as symptoms of a dangerous disease. The music of the people had become anesthetizing; it was a tranquilizing drug, deadening the spirits of the people to the voice of God. It was not the practice of worship nor the use of music but the abuse and misuse of them which the prophets condemned, and rightly so.

Sixth, the practice of worship and the use of music in the Old Testament provided the context out of which came practices of worship and song in the early church. Worship and song form one of the bridges that connect the "old" and the "new."

Music and Worship in the New Testament

Many of the forms and practices of worship in the New Testament were borrowed from the structures and content of worship already in existence in the Jewish synagogue. The components of synagogue worship have already been discussed. Since many of the early Christians were Jews, it is obvious that they would bring into their new faith their Jewish background, which was steeped in tradition and meaning. For the first few decades there was not even an official break between Judaism and the Christian religion. The link between Judaism and Christianity was the belief in the one God who had created heaven and earth.

(This link is very important in our understanding of the relationship between Judaism and the emerging faith.)

The components of worship in the early church were patterned after elements found in the religious services of the synagogue. Keeping in mind the influence of the synagogue, let me note briefly the foundations that undergirded the meaning and manner of New Testament worship.

Characteristics of Worship in the New Testament

The early Christians worshiped on the first day of the week, which came to be known as Sunday (sun day), as opposed to the sabbath of the Jews. The fact that the Christians chose the first day of the week, the day Christ had risen from the dead, is crucial in understanding the faith and worship of the early Christian church. Oscar Cullmann says:

> The Lord's Day of the first Christians was therefore a celebration of Christ's resurrection. *Each* Lord's Day was an Easter Festival, since this was not yet confined to one single Sunday in the year. . . . We are dealing here with a specifically Christian festival day, and the fact that it derives its meaning from Christ's resurrection, gives us an important hint as to the basic Christian meaning of all gatherings of the primitive community for worship.[1]

Where did the early Christians meet for worship? Those in Jerusalem met in the upper room (perhaps the home of the mother of John Mark) and in private homes. Believers elsewhere also met in private homes. However, it must be kept in mind that the whole community of faith gathered together in one place. The community probably gathered daily, although the first day of the week was designated as the day for religious services.

Ferdinand Hahn gives five principles necessary for understanding New Testament worship: (1) "The Christian community assembles for worship on the basis of God's eschatological saving act in Christ, which demonstrates its present power in the operation of the Holy Spirit"; (2) "in worship the . . . edifying . . . of the church takes place"; (3) "for the Christian community worship does not take place in a separate realm but in the midst of the existing world"; (4) "worship can be properly ordered only when the freedom necessary for the operation of the Spirit remains"; and (5) "the worship of Christians is dominated by God's eschatological gift of salvation, and remains open to God's future acts."[2]

Although instruction (preaching) was a component in both the synagogue and the church, the content of that instruction has now changed. Preaching has now become Christ centered. Likewise, although prayer was an element in both the synagogue and the church, the context has once again been changed. Now the prayer is Maranatha: "Come, Lord Jesus." The breaking of bread now looks forward to the messianic banquet of the Lord.

Hymnlike References in the New Testament

Now that observations concerning worship among the New Testament churches have been made, it is necessary to look more specifically into the nature and function of music. A discussion of music has been deliberately held off since it can be understood only in the context of worship.

There is a scattering of references to music in the gospels. What is called the Magnificat (Luke 1:46-55) is a song modeled from the song of Hannah (1 Samuel 2:1-10). The Psalm of Zechariah (Luke 1:68-79), also called the Benedictus, was also borrowed from the Old Testament. The Gloria in Excelsis (Luke 2:14) and Nunc Dimittis (Luke 2:29-32) are hymnic in composition and were found in the worship services of the early church.

It is commonly accepted that Ephesians 5:14 was a baptismal hymn. Of course, the obvious question becomes,

What standard can be used to identify a passage as having a hymnic quality? Ralph Martin offers the following:

> Scholars have looked for passages which have a lyrical quality and rhythmical style, an unusual vocabulary which is different from the surrounding context of the letter in which the passage appears, some distinctive piece of Christian doctrine (usually associated with the Person and work of our Lord Jesus Christ) and hints that the passage in question finds its natural setting in a baptismal or Communion service.[3]

Using this standard, other passages having hymnic characteristics may also be identified, such as 1 Timothy 3:16; Philippians 2:6-11; and Hebrews 1:3. Cullmann sees doxologies as well as other Christ hymns in the book of Revelation. (See also Revelation 4:11; 5:9-10, 12-13.)

Just as there are, in the Old Testament, prophetic outcries against the abuses in worship, so there are, in the New Testament, traces of repudiation against the misuse of worship and music. Romans 12 and 1 Corinthians 14 seem to fit this mold. These passages are concerned with practical guidelines for proper behavior in public worship.

Psalms, Hymns, and Spiritual Songs

Up to this point the concern has been with hymnlike passages in the New Testament. What about specific exhortations to "sing unto the Lord"? In Ephesians 5:19 and Colossians 3:16 the church is instructed to "speak to one another with psalms, hymns and spiritual songs. Sing and make music in your heart to the Lord, always giving thanks to God the Father for everything, in the name of our Lord Jesus Christ" (Ephesians 5:19, NIV). The context of these verses suggests that the writer is showing the Christian the proper way to live. He contrasts the Christian life with the life of those who are given to "darkness." In Colossians the author offers options to "falsehood," which are lowliness, meekness, patience, and forebearance. It is within the context of the new life in Christ that the church is admonished to "address one another in psalms and hymns and spiritual songs."

There has been some debate over the distinction between psalms and hymns and spiritual songs. Gerhard Delling takes the view that psalms, hymns, and spiritual songs "were used without any kind of distinction; if they did not signify distinct types in Christian worship, it is possible that the difference in the context was also expressed in the form."[4]

Eric Routley makes a distinction between the three terms. He sees "psalms" to be a reference to the psalms of the Old Testament and "hymns" to be "new compositions celebrating the resurrection of Christ." According to Routley, the "spiritual songs" may have been an "improvised folk song that naturally grows out of a group which is sharply separated from the rest of the society and which has a strong sense of inner unity."[5]

Paul reminds the Corinthians, "When you come together, each one has a hymn, a lesson, a revelation, a tongue, or an interpretation" (1 Corinthians 14:26). It is possible that the service began with a hymn and that the statement "each one has a hymn" may mean that individuals sang their own hymns or shared them with the congregation.

The Attitude of Jesus Toward Worship

So far no mention has been made of Jesus' attitude toward worship. Certainly, since he was a Jew, raised in the tradition of his people, he was a part of that great tradition. Perhaps as a child, he joined the pilgrims as they traveled to Jerusalem at the time of the feasts with Psalm 121 on his lips. Perhaps he joined in with his disciples in the upper room as they sang the "Hallel" (Psalm 136) at the last supper.

Jesus acted upon his own authority and took his message to the temple and synagogue, but he did not confine his activity to the place of worship. He healed on the sabbath, putting human need above ritual. In the Gospel of John, Jesus gave a Samaritan woman a lesson in the true meaning of worship. "Yet a time is coming and has now come when the true worshipers will worship the Father in spirit and truth, for they are the kind of worshipers the Father seeks" (John 4:23, NIV).

From this it can be seen that it was Jesus himself who gave to the early Christians a "new song," given so frequently in the book of Revelation:

> Then I heard every creature in heaven and on earth and under the earth and on the sea, and all that is in them, singing:
> "To him who sits on the throne and to the Lamb
> be praise and honor and glory and power,
>   forever and ever!"
> The four living creatures said, "Amen," and the elders fell down and worshiped (Revelation 5:13-14, NIV).

Motifs of New Testament Worship

What, then, are some of the important motifs that run through the New Testament in terms of music and worship? First, there is a pronounced richness in the variety of forms in the New Testament. It was mentioned at the outset that, in a sense, it is misleading to speak of the New Testament church; rather, it is more accurate to speak of the churches of the New Testament. The New Testament reveals not one form of worship but several. Distinctions in worship forms existed among the early Aramaic-speaking community, the Hellenistic Jewish community, the early Gentile community, and the sub-apostolic period. This multiplicity of forms suggests that not only between churches but also within each church existed a freedom and spontaneity, devoid of the formality and rigidity that would later characterize Christian worship.

Second, this freedom and spontaneity were a result of

how the early Christians were guided by the Holy Spirit.

Third, there comes the note of celebration. Worship in the New Testament was an act of celebration; therefore, the music of the early church was the music of celebration. The reason the early Christians gathered was to celebrate the victory of the risen Lord. They gathered to "sing a new song," and the song grew out of the *kerygma*. It was this festive climate that characterized the entire activity of the early Christians as they sought to proclaim their faith in a hostile, pagan world.

Fourth, the free working of the Holy Spirit must be viewed in the context of restrictions. The apostle Paul saw the act of worship as serving one end: to build up the family of God. Paul sought to harmonize the freedom of the Spirit with liturgical restrictions by using the guiding principle of edification (1 Corinthians 14:3-4).

This matter of building up the people of God is essential if music and worship are to be placed in their proper context. It is a point to which further attention shall be given and which cannot be ignored if the task is to observe critically the state of music in the black church and offer possible correctives.

That which distinguishes the worship of the Old Testament from that of the early church is obviously the person and work of Jesus Christ. Ultimately, the aim of worship is to be confronted by Jesus of Nazareth, who is the only begotten Son of God and the Lord of the church. It is through the act of worship that the church is empowered to do his will.

CHAPTER THREE

Music and Worship
in Afro-American Culture

We shall now examine the historical context out of which music and worship in the black church have evolved. The examination must begin in Africa, for to begin elsewhere would be similar to making an attempt to study worship and music as practiced in the New Testament churches without looking carefully at the practice of worship in the Old Testament.

At one time scholars such as E. Franklin Frazier argued that African influence on the lives and religion of blacks was minimal. They thought that the Euro-American culture was the primary and dominant force shaping the religion and the very lives of black people in America.

Henry Mitchell takes the view that "Black preaching and Black Religion generally are . . . inescapably the product of the confluence of two streams of culture, one West African and the other Euro-American."[1] Many scholars agree with Mitchell that African culture shaped the music, life-style, thought patterns, and the world view of those Africans transported from the freedom of their homeland through the middle passage to the slavery of the New World.

The Negro Spirituals

This brings us to a discussion of the most celebrated musical contribution of the Afro-American—the Negro spirituals. Note that spirituals are a distinctly American contribution, not born in Africa. Emerging out of the experience of a people in slavery, the spirituals told the story of a disenfranchised people. The spirituals expressed the full range of human emotion: pain, fear, joy, sorrow, despair, hope, futility, and faith.

These "sorrow songs" as spirituals are also called, told the bittersweet story of hardship and struggle. The music of the slaves became the medium by which they were able to survive. The slaves never accepted slavery, and the spirituals, punctuated with hope, are testimonies of the yearning within human souls to be free.

There have been different opinions concerning the meaning of the spirituals. Some writers emphasize the code meaning of many spirituals. Others, such as Benjamin E. Mays, note the other-worldly emphasis in the spirituals. My purpose is not to debate the issue of the meaning of spirituals. The important fact to remember is that the music of the spirituals was a means of "African survival." Important in this discussion is the fact that spirituals were a cultural and theological cry of a people.

It must be kept in mind that just as rhythm was the basic component of African music, rhythm was also basic to the music of spirituals.

Wyatt Tee Walker identifies some basic characteristics of the spiritual form. They are: (a) deep biblicism, (b) eternality of message, (c) rhythm, (d) improvisational, (e) antiphonal, or call and response, (f) double or coded meaning, (g) repetitive, and (h) unique imagery. It might be noted that these same characteristics can be found in the religious music of blacks today. Walker notes the heavy "Jesus theme" emphasis in black religious music and the popularity of music that expresses dependency upon God

(Jesus). Historically, the religious music of black people has been highly Christocentric.[2]

Meter Hymns

Two other developments in the history of the religious music of black people will be noted. First is the influence of the songs of Dr. Isaac Watts, a minister and physician who, along with the Wesley brothers and others, made a great impact upon church music. More than any others, these songs forged a new direction by moving away from psalm singing to religious poem singing. This phenomenon, known as meter singing, is different from the common meter singing during the Great Awakening. Wendell Whalum notes that

> Black Methodists and Baptists endorsed Watts' hymns, but the Baptists "blackened" them. They virtually threw out the meter signature and rhythm and before 1875 had begun a new system which, though based on the style of singing coming from England to America in the eighteenth century, was drastically different from it. It was congregational singing much like the spiritual had been in which the text was retained. . . . When Christianity seized the Black experience the worshippers took hold of whatever was shared with them and made it into a music of their own. This was not plagiarism. It was an honest effort to give God their best. Many spirituals of this period became a part of many hymns.[3]

The worship leader (usually the preacher or deacon) would "line out" the hymn, and the congregation would sing it. This would be followed by the "moaning" (humming) of the stanza. It must be remembered that during this time (1800s) illiteracy was widespread and the use of hymnals virtually nonexistent.

Therefore, the popularity of the meter style hymns was compatible with the social context of the day. These hymns of eight and six lines were easy to remember and fit very well the spirit of the "invisible church" becoming "visible" as black churches began springing up in both the North and South.

Gospel Music

The second development is a type of music that attracts more people perhaps than any other: gospel music. Now obviously blacks are not the only cultural group claiming to utilize such music. There are gospel choirs, and there is gospel music in white churches as well. It might be added that "amens" and shouting can be heard in white churches as well as in black churches. However, just as there is a distinction between the way blacks and whites respond to the worship experience, there is also a difference in the style, tone, and structure of gospel music sung in their churches. Gospel music refers to a certain feeling, tone, and freedom of improvisation that allows the black singer to sing the same song differently each time it is sung, not to be bound by written music. Gospel music in the black church has a distinct sound and spontaneity all its own.

Gospel music has made a great impact upon the music of the black experience in America. However, the contemporary black church, still the most powerful and influential force within the black community, must continually correct those influences that tend to rob the church of its ability to heal the wounds of God's people and restore health to the spiritually and culturally oppressed.

Gospel music, as sung in black churches, is a product of the depression era of the 1930s and 1940s. It would be helpful to use Walker's distinction between "historical gospel" and "modern gospel." Historical refers to that period influenced by Thomas A. Dorsey and others, and modern refers to the period embracing the last twenty-five years.

Just as the spirituals and meter hymns had been, so gospel music emerged as a social indicator of a historical moment. This music was born in hard times and was fueled by the experiences of a people only seventy years this side of slavery. A simultaneous musical form called the "blues" emerged from a musical form known as "ragtime." The blues were a secular comment on social and economic conditions of the times. The words were different, although the feelings and experiences were the same.

Walker also speaks of the social significance of gospel music:

> The creation of Gospel music is a social statement that, in the face of America's rejection and economic privation, Black folks made a conscious decision to be themselves. It was an early stage of identity awakening and identity nourishing. It signaled a return to "roots."[4]

The Nature of Music in the Black Experience

From this survey of the religious music of the Afro-American, some conclusions can be drawn concerning the nature and function of music in the black experience.

First, there is an evident and an undeniable connection between African music and the music of black Americans. This connection is seen in the way in which slaves continued to sing "their" songs in a strange land. They borrowed songs from the white world and shaped them to fit their need.

Second, the world view of the African was a holistic world view, which was given full expresssion in the way music was woven into the very fabric of life.

Third, music was the common denominator that allowed slaves brought to the New World to communicate in the language of one spirit. It was the form of their yearnings and hopes.

Fourth, the context out of which the music came was the "invisible church," the secret meetings and gatherings in which blacks could be themselves and "sing the Lord's song in a strange land." Thus, the black church was born and became the most powerful force in the black community.

Fifth, in each instance blacks "blackened" worship, and the worship experience became the single, most-important event in their weekly cycle of human encounters.

Sixth, black folk worship, highly spontaneous and flexible, moved to the rhythm of the Holy Spirit. As Jesus found blacks and as blacks found Jesus, there was always time for celebration on Sunday morning, for it was at the meeting that they could tell Jesus all about their struggles.

Black Music and the Biblical Norm

The biblical standard demands that music be understood and used within the context of worship. Worship is the corporate celebration of what God has done through Jesus Christ and his continuing presence through the work and power of the Holy Spirit. In worship, confronted by God, comforted by his grace, and made uncomfortable by his judgment, the worshiper confesses sins and accepts God's forgiveness.

In the black church, purpose was also found in the midst of oppression. In worship blacks had a good time. They affirmed who they were as well as who God is. They cast burdens on the altar. They were reminded that each of them was somebody. They fellowshiped with members of their extended families. They received power to go on a little while longer. Such is the historical meaning of worship in the black experience.

This meaning has been carried out through music. However, one must be careful not to reduce music to a mere exercise in self-aggrandizement. A distinction must be made between celebrating and parading, between lifting Jesus and lifting self. Worship is degrading when it is turned into a circus and when attention is turned on each other's performance rather than focused on Christ who is the reason for celebration.

Another way in which music has been abused and separated from historical underpinnings is by its disconnection from the larger context of the black church's mission. Even though people may be attracted by the worship and music of the church, worship and music must be seen as a means rather than an end. There is a correlation between the dominant type of music sung by a church and the church's self-perception of mission and ministry. Black preachers are constantly reminding their congregations that religion is more than Sunday worship. Worship is abused when the activity of God is confined to the Sunday morning hour. If all energy is placed into singing music that has no relationship to everyday life, then the purpose of worship is forfeited, and the worshiper becomes disconnected from the way music and worship have served blacks historically.

Still another way in which the historical meaning of worship and music has been uprooted is by separating black theology from music. Olin Moyd defines black theology as

> the Black community's attempt to reflect upon the historical relationship—events—between God and themselves. . . . Black theology seeks to explicate the Black community's understanding of God's promise and the goal toward which he is directing the world while Black people in America are and were going through dehumanizing experiences.[5]

The subject matter of black theology and, therefore, the content of black music have come from within the black community. Although the religious poems of the meter hymns were written by whites, the poems spoke the language of black suffering and hope and, at the same time, were recast into the black idiom.

Today, part of the problem is that much of the music sung is assembly-line manufactured, packaged, and labeled and distributed to the churches via the radio and the record shop. Much of this music is written and sung commercially by persons who lack depth in their own religious experience and who spin off songs in order to fill albums for distribution. These songs are sung by choirs, many of whom have no connection with the black church. Such songs have a fleeting popularity on the top ten music charts and soon fade into oblivion, only to be replaced by more songs of the same tone and quality. Local church choirs take this "packaged" music and attempt to duplicate the sound and substance of each selection, thereby destroying the possibility for their own creativity and spontaneity so characteristic of the black heritage.

Although it is commendable that through modern technology black religious music has been lifted from obscurity and neglect, black religious music should not be used primarily to satisfy the material appetites of record companies.

The quality of music must be constantly tested by the biblical norm. First, music must be understood in the context of worship. Second, music must reflect the social as well as the theological history of the community. Third, worship must always hold spontaneity and discipline in constant tension. Fourth, a primary test of the components of worship is whether or not the components in question contribute to the edification, or "up-building," of the people of God. Fifth, music in the synagogue and the early church was only one of the components of worship. Sixth, worship confronts the people of God in the Old Testament with the Spirit of the Almighty and in the New Testament with the activity of this same God in Jesus Christ, who enables people to discern and do his will.

In the following chapters the various areas and relationships in the church with reference to the music program are examined and guidelines are offered to improve the qualitative use of music in the black church.

CHAPTER FOUR

Music in the Various Contexts of Worship

Before speaking of the relationship between music and worship, one must return to the biblical model. First, worship, especially as reflected in the New Testament, had a variety of forms, resulting from the responses of the many cultural and social groups that embraced the Christian faith. Second, worship in the New Testament and to a degree in the Old Testament, was a spontaneous act, and this spontaneity was reflected in the manner in which early Christians were guided by the Holy Spirit in the free expression of their newfound faith. Third, worship in the New Testament was an act of celebration. The early Christians gathered first and foremost to celebrate the resurrection of Jesus, who is the Christ and Lord of the church. Fourth, the early Christians, although under the influence and guidance of the Holy Spirit, always maintained boundaries of religious expression. The apostle Paul used the guiding principle of edification, for his primary concern was the building up of the people of God.

Worship, then, is a corporate demonstration of belief and faith in God through adoration and praise, an attempt of the human spirit to touch the divine through religious activity. Worship is the celebration of the mighty acts of God, who has moved in history, confronting the worshiper in a corporate and personal manner. Christian worship is the celebration of God's love completely and fully demonstrated in the life of his son, Jesus Christ, and his ultimate triumph over the reality of sin and evil.

Because of the historical circumstances of black people, worship in the black tradition has reflected a particular tone and texture, some characteristics of which were described earlier. Yet these particularities are rooted in the divine-human encounter as dialogue: God talks, and persons listen. The black theologian J. Deotis Roberts describes this same encounter from a black viewpoint when he says, "Man cries, God hears."[1] The black religious experience has been shaped by the attempt of a slave people to "sing the Lord's song in a strange land," which, in fact, they did!

As a result of sociological and cultural factors already identified, worship among the masses of black people has mirrored historical developments. The religion of the black masses is emotional and festive. As a result, music in black churches has reflected a particular emotional tone and an other-worldly emphasis. The black church has always adapted to the needs of the times, and today it is helpful to review periodically and analyze critically the music that is supposed to reflect the divine-human encounter at its best.

The variety of musical forms within the black idiom needs to be appreciated. The worship service should not be dominated by a single type of music.

The dominant type in most black churches is gospel music. These songs should be chosen with care. They must not be used indiscriminately. Often the theology of the lyrics of many gospel songs reflects a self-centeredness that has no place in worship. Some songs speak of God as a kind of cosmic Santa Claus, showering his children with blessings upon request. Rather than dwelling upon God's responsibility toward the worshiper, church music, as well as the worship experience, should focus upon responsibility toward God.

Another type of music in worship is the spiritual. Take note of the cry of the oppressed community echoed in the words of this spiritual:

> Oh! Nobody knows the trouble I've seen,
> Nobody knows but Jesus.
> Nobody knows the trouble I've seen
> Glory, hallelujah.

Notice the recognition of the present reality of suffering and pain and at the same time a firm conviction that God will reverse the situation. In this one spiritual there is both a note of despair and hope: "Nobody knows . . . but Jesus. . . . trouble . . . Glory, hallelujah."

Spirituals should be used in worship, for they are commentaries on the past as well as wellsprings of hope for the future. As stated earlier, the Negro spiritual is a distinctly American contribution made by Afro-Americans.

The Negro spiritual maintains the delicate balance between this-worldly and other-worldly theology. Roberts thinks that the use of Negro spirituals in worship would serve as a corrective to gospel music. He states:

> The spirituals came out of our slavery experience. They had the advantage over gospel music of being both this-worldly as well as otherworldly. Perhaps it would be useful for us to sing spirituals along with gospel songs and to seek to interpret both—that is, to provide the social-historical context as well as the Biblical and theological message of both forms of black music.[2]

Each worship service must include hymns. According to the *Harvard Dictionary of Music*, a hymn is defined simply as "a song of praise or adoration of God."[3] The best hymns are universal in describing this divine-human relationship. One should study the different types of hymns, for example, adoration, praise, meditation, departure. The stanzas of hymns comprise units of thought woven together. Therefore, in order to get the full impact of the hymn, all stanzas should be sung. The hymn calls for congregational participation. Because of the tendency of the congregation to slow the tempo, the organist should play the hymn in its entirety at the proper tempo before the congregation begins to sing.

Austin Lovelace writes of the importance of introducing the hymn.

> Many organists play over a hymn tune before the congregation starts singing as if it were a matter of small or no importance. . . . Yet, the introduction is a most important factor in good hymn playing.
> The first job of the introduction is to give the correct tempo.[4]

The congregation should be made aware that the organist is attempting to establish the tempo.

The hymn offers an opportunity for variety in performance. The first stanza of the hymn may be sung in unison, the second stanza without musical accompaniment, the third stanza in parts, and other variations.

However, any kind of variation should not be overdone. Jack Goode states:

> While it is not only possible but a very excellent idea to sing an occasional hymn stanza entirely unaccompanied, this must be done with care. . . . To start with you need a familiar hymn, and you should employ unaccompanied singing only where it seems suitable to the text. Use your choir as a firm guide for the congregation.[5]

As stated earlier, because the standard hymn is a religious poem and expresses a complete idea, each stanza should be sung. The organist may wish to use improvisation as well as modulation in an effort to be creative and imaginative.

Hymns should be appreciated for their authorship as well as for the existential and sociological context out of which they were composed. Black congregations, especially, should be knowledgeable of the contributions of black composers, such as Charles Tindley, E. C. Deas, Lucie Campbell, and Dr. and Mrs. A. M. Townsend; as well as arrangers, such as R. Nathaniel Dett, John W. Work, Sr., Hall Johnson, and William Dawson. The contributions of these composers of Afro-American descent have been well documented by Eileen Southern and others, and the study of their lives and works should be part of the religious education curriculum of every black church.

One of the musical forms rapidly disappearing in the black church is the singing of meter hymns, which were discussed earlier. Meter singing has been one of the most beautiful and moving expressions of religious faith ever created. This style of singing is done without musical accompaniment, which underscores the fact that instruments, although desirable, are not essential to worship.

Blacks borrowed the hymns of Watts, Wesley, and others, threw out the original meter, and made them into unique expressions of faith. This form must be retained, since the responsibility of the black church is not only to create but to preserve. These meter hymns, passed down through generations, must be taught as part of music education in the black church. Perhaps they can be re-popularized by black college choirs, traditional repositories of the black music tradition. The black college choirs also popularized Negro spirituals a century ago.

Musical Instruments in Worship

The organ and piano have been the traditional musical instruments in the black church for worship. In the rural black churches, particularly in the South, at the turn of the century, instruments were scarce. Gradually, pianos could be found in these churches. Organs came into prominence in larger southern cities and increasingly in the industrialized urban areas of the North.

With the rise in popularity of gospel music, black

churches began purchasing organs, which seemed well suited for the gospel style of singing. Today, these organs are equipped with all kinds of extras, including percussions sounds such as drums. It should be noted that the use of this kind of organ was more popular in the black churches of the masses than in the middle-class institutional churches of the North. In the educated black congregations of the South, the pipe organ or an electronic organ with a pipe organ sound was, and still is, the rule rather than the exception. In fact, many black congregations have rebelled against the superficial bland sound of the electronic organ and its "ballroom" tone.

The selection of a church organ is one of the most important decisions a congregation will ever make. An organ is not a frequent purchase. Therefore, the congregation will probably be forced to live with the purchase for a long time. It is essential that the minister, organist, and members of the organ committee obtain a reasonable amount of expertise in the area of organ selection. Often, electronic organ salespersons are biased and assume that a certain brand is desirable. It is important to remember that the selection of an organ should reflect the congregation's appreciation of the best in the black music heritage and the variety of musical offerings.

If a committee is chosen to select a new organ or piano, the members of that committee should have some background and guidelines. If the congregation does not have qualified persons, help can be sought from outside resources, for example, the music department of a black college. There are many alternatives to the artificial sound of the electronic organs that unfortunately floods so many churches. It is sad that much more consideration and attention are given to other church purchases than to this important purchase. Even though the price and maintenance cost of a pipe organ may be prohibitive, other selections are available and well suited for the budget of the average black church.

Care should also be used in the selection of a church piano. The same expertise necessary for the selection of an organ is needed for the selection of a piano. It is most important to remember that a piano suited for the den at home is not adequate for a church sanctuary, which demands a heavier, richer sounding, more durable instrument.

Other Instruments

In the black churches of the masses other instruments, notably drums and tambourines, are becoming increasingly popular. Preparations for many church services are reminiscent of the preparation made before night club performances, as musicians "set the stage" and test the microphones and instruments before the "performance" begins.

The Bible cannot be used to condone or condemn the use of instruments. The Old Testament has been used to justify their use, while the New Testament has been used to justify their nonuse. Some churches have used the references to the use of instruments in the Old Testament as an excuse to be excessive. Others use the silence of the New Testament relative to the use of instruments as a reason to ban instruments entirely from the worship service.

The purpose of the instrument is to accompany the songs of the people of God. The musician uses the instrument to make his or her music offering to God in the context of the community of worshipers. It is not the use of other instruments but their misuse that is of concern. The drum, if used to evoke emotion through the accent on rhythm, should be avoided. It must not be assumed that the drum is the only instrument worthy of consideration. It would be more advisable to incorporate trumpets and other brass instruments during hymn renditions as well as stringed instruments during special music offerings. These instruments might also be considered for use when the church choirs present seasonal concerts of sacred music, such as during Advent and Lent.

The Christian Wedding

The wedding has always taken on religious significance, for it represents one of life's important transitions. It symbolizes the movement from the family of procreation to the family of orientation. It represents another beginning. It is an event that alters and reshapes a human life and places that life within the context of a sharing relationship. For many centuries the church has been invited to preside over the ceremony that unites two individuals.

However, the church, for most of its history, did not perform weddings. The question of whether the church should perform the wedding is answered by James White who suggests that "the best argument in its favor seems to be that the church as a community of faith has an intimate concern in surrounding a Christian couple with love and in ministering to them."[6]

Christian marriage must be seen within the context of the belief that the marriage relationship is of God and that God's presence is invoked in the exchanging of vows in the sanctuary as others witness this transitional event. It is essential that the spiritual nature of marriage is affirmed and that the ceremony is placed in the confines of Christian worship. A church wedding is a worship service. In this worship service God's presence is invoked. The wedding ceremony is not merely for the bride nor for any human participant. The service should point to God and his sovereignty over the whole of life. It is God whose presence is made known in the transitions of life.

Couples seeking a church wedding should be counseled and taught the meaning and purpose of the marriage ceremony. The wedding ceremony belongs to the church and not to the couple. The pastor should seek to guide each couple in their understanding of the components and content of such a service. The sacred quality of the service should be stressed.

White says:

> Most Christian couples are open to suggestions as to how to make their wedding the finest possible act of Christian worship. The priest or minister must be familiar with the options available. . . . This is more demanding of pastoral leadership but also provides a better opportunity for ministering.[7]

The music of the service should always maintain the integrity and worshipful nature of the ceremony. The selection of music, although made in consultation with the couple, should always reflect a sacred quality. The pastor must assert authority to direct and shape the ceremony and liturgy of the church.

Wedding music should not be chosen on the basis of the personal preferences of the bride or the family. The marriage service is no place for "pop" or secular songs. The theme of wedding music should not be human love but, rather, God's love, which is given expression in human love. The wedding reception offers a better setting in which to use music that does not invoke and invite the divine presence.

Some ministers may wish to compromise by allowing the personal preferences of the participants to be sung before the ceremony begins and insisting that music offered during the ceremony bear a distinct sacred tone. In maintaining the sacred quality of the marriage ceremony through the proper use of music, the church is affirming the fact that in the act of marriage, God is present and that his presence is indeed meaningful. Perhaps the couple may then be influenced to allow God's presence permanent residence in their continuing relationship.

The Christian Funeral

Death is another of life's transitions. It is the final event of life. The human soul ponders the meaning of life but also confronts the inevitability of death. Religion raises questions and at the same time offers some answers to the mystery of life and the certainty of death. The church affirms that God stands at both the beginning and ending of life.

Historically, the funeral in the black church is an event. Particularly in the black churches of the masses the funeral has served a social and psychological as well as a theological function. In African society, music was an important part of the funeral ritual. In the slave community death was a celebration of the end of the slave's earthly struggle. Even today, the funeral is a meaningful and sometimes elaborate ritual in the black community.

One might raise the question of the purpose of the funeral. Andrew Blackwood maintains that "the chief aim is to glorify God."[8] James White lists two concerns as the Christian community seeks to understand the function of the funeral: "to show forth God's love and the community's support in consoling the bereaved, and to commend the deceased to God's gracious care."[9] The purpose, then, is not to foster a kind of superficial emotionalism nor to pay one's last respects. Neither is it a sentimental send-off to Paradise, "We loved you, but God loved you best." Of course, God loves best because his love is perfect. However, God does not cause pain merely because "he wants another flower in his garden." God is not callous and unloving; yet funeral services, as well as funeral music, frequently become warmed-over exercises in the sentimental.

James White says, "God's words in scripture and actions in sacraments are the strong medicine needed at this time, not poetry, flowers, or sentimental statements."[10] Families should not be allowed to choose hymns and other songs without receiving guidance in evaluating the theological assumptions of such music.

The Christian church affirms that the Christian funeral is also a worship service. Death must be dealt with realistically as it is placed in the context of worship. The funeral must deal with God as well as with human grief. Paul Irion suggests:

> Since the funeral is recognized as a religious rite, a portion of its attention is turned toward God. Its purpose is to present a vision of God which will be of comfort and help to the mourners in their suffering.[11]

Two cautions must be offered here. On the one hand, the notion of grief without hope should be avoided. On the other hand, the reality of death must be accepted. The funeral service should aid the community in doing both. It is a celebration of life. In the service the congregation petitions God to strengthen and sustain those who mourn. This captures the spirit of the early church. The context of Christian burial in the early church was the hope of the resurrection. This dual note of hope and celebration should continue to set the tone for the funeral service in the black tradition.

Selecting appropriate music can do a great deal to enhance the funeral service and to invoke the presence of God upon those who mourn. There is no need for the organ to be played throughout the service. Neither is it desirable for soloists or choirs to sing old sentimental favorites that may encourage emotionalism. Hymns should have a resurrection theme, for it is during the experience of death that the Christian finds hope in the resurrection of Christ. Songs of strength, comfort, and assurance that focus on God rather than human sentiments should be utilized.

Because of the emotional tone of the mourners, care should be taken to ensure that the family in mourning understands what the funeral should mean and how that meaning can best be served. This also involves education and training.

It must be remembered that death is a crisis situation. Edward Wimberly places such crises in the context of pastoral care in the black church. He says, "Moreover, crises present opportunities for the black church to draw upon its traditions in assisting in the nurturing task of educating the congregation."[12]

Perhaps workshops should be held to bring people to a better understanding, not only of the purpose and meaning of the funeral, but also of the purpose and role of the church at a time of death. (The occurrence of death is not the only appropriate time to talk about death.) In such a learning session persons can understand the function of the funeral and funeral music and the appropriateness of nontraditional hymns, anthems, and even Negro spirituals. When the funeral is placed within the meaningful context of worship, the church will be able to proclaim more effectively Christ as the Lord of life.

CHAPTER FIVE

The Pastor

Any discussion of issues relating to music in the black church must of necessity begin with the pastor. The pastor stands at the head of the local church in terms of its organizational and ecclesiastical functioning. He or she has been entrusted with the care of God's people. This is true not only in an ecclesiastical sense but also in a theological one. The pastor, although not necessarily a trained theologian, assumes a particular theological insight. Pastors may not be the only persons in their congregations with theological sensitivity. But they, more than anyone else, have been given authority to make some sense out of what God expects of his people.

Pastors seek to interpret and articulate the Word of God in light of the traditions and doctrines of faith. They have been entrusted with the care of souls. These responsibilities are not to be taken lightly. The way in which pastors direct the total ministry of the church will help to determine the content and relevance of that ministry.

Particularly is this true in the black church. The black pastor has been given much authority to direct and influence the total life of the local black church. Because of the importance blacks have traditionally given to the black church, the black minister, for good or ill, has been seen as the single most important person in the black church and in the community as well.

It has been well documented, and it has already been noted, that the black church became the most important institution within the black community. In African culture, the priest was given a place of honor and respect. This survival of an African custom has placed a great burden upon black pastors, for often their expertise in many areas of pastoring is more imagined than real. Congregations can more easily come to terms with pastoral strengths and weaknesses when pastors themselves come to terms with them. One pastor may be stronger in the preaching area than in administration. Another may be sensitive in the area of counseling but weak in program planning. Each minister must assess his or her own strengths and weaknesses and seek to improve the weak areas.

James Massey calls attention to the diversity of pastoral gifts. He says,

> Every [pastor] has his proper gift, and time and place for using it. Some men have an aptness for administration; they can bring managerial techniques to bear upon church life, project plans, and dispense papers throughout committees and parish families. . . . Some others excel at delicate relations, counseling, sustaining. . . . Some others will excel at preaching.[1]

Added to these routine pastoral burdens is the obvious dilemma faced by the black preacher: "It is no secret that for several centuries in American life the black preacher has had to provide a strong spiritual leadership wedded to a strong social concern."[2]

Music: A Sensitive Pastoral Area

One of the weak areas of pastoral ministry is the area of church music. To a large extent, many pastors take a hands-off approach to the whole area of the music ministry of the church. There are perhaps two reasons for this. First, most pastors feel ill equipped to deal with issues relating to music practices in the church. Second, the music department in the church has long been a potential trouble spot, and many ministers fear that any interference would be like stirring up a hornet's nest.

Both misconceptions should be corrected. A minister does not necessarily need any special musical training or expertise; the musician has, or should have, the necessary preparation in the field. Furthermore, one may indeed be the recipient of specialized training in the area of church music and still not possess the sensitivity and ability to deal with issues affecting the form and function of music in the total ministry of the church.

This has to do with theology, for it is theology that informs our music. For instance, if the only purpose of music is to arouse the worshiper emotionally, that says something about the content of the theology. When the worship service is allowed to become unbalanced and entertainment oriented, a certain theological statement is being made.

The pastor is the person who should be able to guide the congregation into a more meaningful worship experience. The pastor does not have to be a trained organist or a professional singer to relate the music of the church to the total church program, but the pastor must be intellectually secure and academically trained.

Second, a pastor needs to understand the reasons why the music department in a church seems to be the perennial "thorn in the flesh." Robert Mitchell suggests that it is important to understand the nature of the choir situation. He says:

> The dynamics that lead to unity or conflict operate with unique intensity because of the characteristic nature of the choir situation. Choir members are probably more continually and frequently engaged in their activity than members of any other group within the church. Normally they meet

at least twice every week, for both rehearsal and ministry. The focus of all these meetings will be upon whatever objective they have determined for themselves. This intensive commitment to a task leads, predictably, to a heightened level of feelings about it. Thus, there is a tendency that if the choir is divisive, it will be strongly; if unified, the unity will be a powerful one.[3]

This is especially true in the black church where position, decision making, and power plays take on an intensity and seriousness that are potentially disruptive. To a large extent, blacks do not have access to position and power in the outside world. These psychological and sociological needs are met within the black church where singing in the choir, as well as other activities, fills a social need to belong and to be recognized. Matters become heated and emotion laden when power and position are threatened. Pastors must understand these dynamics if they are to be effective in dealing with underlying dysfunctional elements.

The pastor must also understand the importance of music in the black church. Though music's importance may be obvious, the extent of its importance is not always appreciated. Because music is significant in the black church, the issues related to it become highly visible. Just as people join the church for different reasons, they also join the choirs for different reasons, and their purposes and goals may be totally different from the stated ministry of the church. It is possible to be a member of a choir without being connected theologically to the body of Christ. Thus the choir runs the risk of being compartmentalized. If there are several choirs in the church—which is the case in most black churches—the problem is multiplied and magnified.

If guidance is sought from the biblical model, one of the themes evident in the New Testament concept of the church must again be restated: the church is the body of Christ. It is not a splintered or dismembered body, but a whole body. Paul spoke of the "edification of the body of Christ" as the basis for worship and ministry.

It is also helpful to view the church as a group of inter-related parts, each finding fulfillment only in relation to the whole. This "systems model" is becoming increasingly helpful in understanding the relationship between the various ministries of the church. From this viewpoint it can be seen that every organization, including the choir(s), is a part of this church system, and what affects the various parts of the system affects the whole.[4]

The Need for Pastoral Leadership

Of course part of the problem is frequently the lack of leadership and guidance, rather than excessive tampering by the pastor. The minister is in a position to place the ministry of music in a larger context.

Therefore, the pastor, as leader, must be involved in the organizational system out of which ministries take shape. The following recommendations are offered, using the biblical model and recognizing the need for meaningful interaction between the pastor and the other components of the system.

First, the pastor should appoint a music committee, if one does not already exist. The music committee should not be confused with the music department. In many black churches, the music department loosely consists of church musicians and heads of choirs. Again, this limited concept tends to maintain the compartmentalization attitude prevalent in much of the church's life.

The music committee concept takes into consideration the accountability and responsibility of the choirs of the church. Therefore, this music committee should be composed of the pastor, a deacon, and one or two church members at large, as well as other persons directly involved in the music component, for example, musicians and choir officers.

Second, the pastor should spend some time in choir rehearsals and meetings. Very often the only time the pastor attends such rehearsals and meetings is when there is an apparent problem. Perhaps a more frequent presence might avoid problems.

The real value and purpose in attending choir rehearsals is educational. In order to evaluate critically the music of the church, some time must be spent teaching the theology found in hymnals and spiritual songs. Some attention should be given to the background of hymns, hymn writers, and the whole field of hymnology and religious poetry upon which present hymnody is based. It might be good for the pastor to lead the choir members in reading the words without music. Some words and phrases are archaic, and their meaning is in need of clarification. Often, more attention is given to the music than to the words and their meanings.

Third, the pastor should encourage the planning and implementation of a music workshop in the local church. The purpose of such a workshop is to make the entire congregation more aware of giving God the best, even the best musically.

The workshop should not be allowed to degenerate into a singing contest or choir festival. It is a learning experience, which may be open to interested persons in other churches. My church recently sponsored such a workshop on a Saturday morning. Classes were offered in hymnology, music theory, elementary conducting, choir issues, and music in the black church. At the conclusion there was an assembly during which one of the instructors played a piece by a black composer whose music had been studied that day.

This workshop not only helped those in attendance become better stewards of the music of the church, but also highlighted the life and work of a black composer other than the more popular ones heard through the media. The enthusiastic response to and large attendance at the workshop underscored the need and desire for more of the same.

For Baptist churches that are members of local associations, such a workshop would provide a needed service. The departments of education in the local associations could offer workshops, lectures, and classes to educate church leaders in this important area of ministry.

Fourth, the pastor must be able to diffuse potential problems within the choir(s) through communication and understanding. He or she must not allow music issues to be confused with choir issues. Of course, the point here is that problems of personality and decision making can spill over into the music ministry. It is important to identify and label the problem. There should be opportunity for dialogue and debate, while keeping all matters within the context of the church's mission.

Fifth, the pastor must not confuse "making a joyful noise unto the Lord" with excessive emotionalism and theatrics, which have no place in the serious worship of God. It has been noted in an earlier chapter that the apostle Paul sought to harmonize the freedom of the Spirit with liturgical restriction by using the guiding principle of edification. Just as Paul saw the need to emphasize moral and ethical boundaries, he also saw and stressed the need for liturgical boundaries.

The minister must teach people the meaning of worship and the relationship of music to the total life of the church. Unfortunately, much of what goes on in the churches has the consent of the minister, even though the minister may privately criticize these excesses in worship. This may be partially due to the pastor's desire to maintain a degree of popularity and "give the people what they want." Certainly this should not be the guiding reason determining what is encouraged or discouraged.

The ministry of the church cannot afford to use gimmicks

and superficial activities to attract the masses. Churches should be built on ministry, not music, and certainly not the type of music that seeks to encourage artificial emotion. The pastor, who is in reality the worship leader, can do much to guide the congregation into a deeper worship experience. This is not intended to be a denial of genuine emotion, which has a legitimate place in the worship tradition. Again, the concern is with the abuse of emotion and the attempt to make emotionalism central to worship.

Sixth, the pastor must consider the philosophy and theology of church music of the musician who is being considered for the position of organist or music director. It is not essential that there be total agreement in terms of theology and objectives. However, if there are irreconcilable differences, tensions will develop that could hinder the ministry of the church. Robert Mitchell warns:

> When the director of the choir operates from different objectives than those of the pastor and/or the church, it is inevitable that dysfunctional tensions will develop. This seems obvious; it would be unreasonable for a church to enter into such a relationship.[5]

The pastor and music committee assigned to select a musician should address themselves to such questions as: Has the candidate had any training? Can he or she read music, select music, and train a choir? Are there recommendations from other churches? What are his or her objectives? Are persons hired because the choir likes them, or because they are qualified and compatible with the total ministry of the church?

Seventh, one of the perennial problems faced by pastors and churches alike is the scarcity of qualified, trained musicians. This scarcity is the lament of both pastors and churches. Of course, one of the reasons for such a shortage of trained musicians and such an abundance of untrained musicians is that churches have, through silence, accepted this condition. If churches' expectations are low, then the kind of musicians churches produce will reflect such expectations.

The black church must lift its standards and demand more of those persons entrusted with the music of the church. The pastor might encourage the idea that monies be spent to train musicians, and the church might include that item in its budget. Piano, organ, and voice lessons could be offered as well as courses in music theory and reading. The church has the resources to train those who will be, in this generation and the next, well trained and competent in the field of church music.

Often musicians and pastors have separated music from theology. As a result, both minister and musician have tended to go separate ways, each confined to his or her own area of familiarity. To avoid this separation, the musician and pastor should become partners in ministry, each offering his or her own skills in the total ministry of the church.

CHAPTER SIX

The Church Musician

The church musician holds a very important position in the life of the church. This is due, in part, to the very nature of the church and the place of worship in its total ministry. Worship is at the center of the life of the church. It has already been noted in a previous chapter that Christian worship was born out of the resurrection event and the need of the first disciples to celebrate the resurrection of the Lord. Since the beginning of Christianity, music has been a part of the worship experience of the church.

It has also been observed that in the black church, worship became an act of celebration and what happened in church on Sunday morning became the most important happening in the lives of black people. Naturally, those persons within the black community who demonstrated certain gifts and unusual talent were given status and recognition by the community.

Since some musicians possessed a special gift that the rest of the community did not possess, they assumed positions of importance within the community, particularly within the black church. Even the musician's ability to play by ear (to play the organ or piano without the ability to read music) was seen by many as a special gift of the Spirit. In the same manner black preachers who did not use a prepared script but who relied upon the power of the Holy Spirit were seen as somehow more authentic agents of the Word than those who prepared sermons.

These two factors, the importance of music in the church and the possession of musical talent by only a few, have contributed to the present situation within the black church, namely, that there is a shortage of qualified musicians to serve. Pastors and churches both agree that good musicians are difficult to find. This is true even in the churches where musicians primarily play by ear and where the singing of gospel music dominates the musical landscape.

With the rise in the popularity of gospel music within the black church came an increased demand for musicians whose only qualification had to be the ability to play by ear. No other training was required or, in some cases, desired. In fact, in many instances training was frowned upon.

Many trained musicians have been frustrated in the local church because of the pressure to teach, not just "some" gospel music, but "all" gospel music. This is especially true for musicians who work with young people who demand the livelier type of music. The preference for this type of music is also influenced by the secular music of our day.

In fact, the music of the secular world has frequently been duplicated in the church; only the lyrics have been changed. But this is not new. The musicologist Gustave Reese demonstrates how composers of the great choral works of the Reformation period borrowed from the secular polyphony of the day. He notes that Johann Sebastian Bach borrowed a *lied* (a German song) melody from a ballet composed by Hans Leo Hassler and used it in his St. Matthew Passion.[1] The name of this now familiar hymn is "O Sacred Head Now Wounded." Love songs, humorous songs, and drinking songs were adapted to religious texts throughout history. Furthermore, the fifteenth century carol sprang from the same source as the ballad; they both were derived from the medieval dance and popularized by the Franciscans, a religious order, for the purpose of spreading their religious teachings.

The Qualifications of the Musician

It is still necessary to deal with the matter of qualifications. Most people would agree that musicians should possess certain qualifications if a standard is to be maintained in terms of the ministry of the church. What should these qualifications be? What should a church desire in a musician? What tools should a musician seek in the development of skills worthy to be offered unto God?

First, musicians must view their positions in terms of the larger ministry of the church. At this point, a distinction must be made between a musician and a "church musician." Obviously, a church musician is a vital part of the church's ministry. He or she is "ministering" music that has been inspired by the very fact of the church's existence.

Church musicians are handling eternal religious truth. They are commenting on the meaning of that truth through music. The music that the musician interprets was not created yesterday. It is just a small part of the church's historical tradition, a tradition that is both greater and more important than the musician or the music he or she plays. The music goes far beyond cultural peculiarities and racial distinctions. It is first and foremost the music of the people of God. A white congregation may set the text of Psalm 27 to the music of a majestic anthem. A black congregation in the rural South may borrow the same text and transform it into black gospel. But the inspiration for both is still the twenty-seventh psalm. The music of the church is a part of the treasure we have in earthen vessels.

This is to say that church musicians are not qualified to handle this music treasure unless they are committed to the larger ministry of the church and, to use again the language of the apostle Paul, the "building up" of the family of God. Too often the church has obtained the services of persons who may possess musical talents but who themselves have not been touched by the music they offer; neither have they demonstrated any commitment, sensitivity, or understanding of the nature and ministry of the church.

Second, church musicians should understand that they work within the framework of the church's total ministry and that the pastor is the head of the overall program and operation of the church. The fact that pastors may not be musicians does not matter. What matters is that pastors are responsible for the church's total ministry which *includes* the music ministry.

Many church musicians have run into problems because they have been unwilling to work under the auspices of the pastoral office. It would be helpful for a musician to consider this pastoral relationship in all of its dimensions before accepting the position of organist, choir director or whatever. The musician and pastor should discuss their relationship, purposes, and goals in order to get a clearer understanding of what is expected. Perhaps a job description could be devised to assist in the clarification of responsibilites and expectations. It would be to the musician's advantage to find out beforehand if the position being offered fits his or her philosophy of music as it relates to the life of the church and the peculiarities of the denomination.

After such deliberations, it would be advantageous if a meeting could be arranged between the pastor, music committee, musician, and the *choir*. It must be clear that the choir does not hire the musician. The musician is under the authority of the church and should be ultimately responsible to the church. However, potential problems would be eliminated if the musician and choir members engaged in meaningful dialogue beforehand. In such a dialogue, expectations, responsibilities, and common purposes could be discussed.

Third, the church musician should know how to read music. Already there is an overabundance of persons with musical talent, but with little musical training. An attempt has already been made to explain how this situation has arisen: partially because musicians themselves have not sought to become better equipped and partially because the black church has not demanded trained musicians. The church musician should not be content with a limited ability, no matter how prestigious is the musical gift of playing by ear. By being content, musicians place limits not only upon themselves but also—and even worse—upon the choir's versatility and the authenticity of the church's worship experience. The musician must constantly evaluate his or her own strengths and weaknesses.

Musical training gives the musician options. A beauty of the black worship experience lies in the freedom to utilize various musical forms, demonstrating the richness and variety of the black experience. A musician who cannot read music limits, rather than fosters, music expression. A church musician who can read music is able to interpret a hymn the way the composer intended and to bring to life an obscure Negro spiritual. A church musician should also have some knowledge of composers and arrangers, especially those who have helped shape the music of black America.

Fourth, the qualified musician should be knowledgeable of the liturgical year and plan the music of the church according to the church calendar. For instance, Christmas music should be seen within the context of the entire Advent and Christmastide season. The musician does not wait until the Sunday before Christmas to offer a Christmas hymn. The season of Advent consists of four Sundays leading up to Christmastide. Christmastide is then followed by Epiphany. The hymn "Joy to the World" is an Epiphany hymn and should be sung during that season of the church year.

The same applies for Easter. Easter cannot be disconnected from the entire Lenten season, which begins as early as Ash Wednesday and continues to Easter. In the church year, Easter is followed by the seasons of Pentecost and Trinity.

An appreciation of the church's liturgical year will allow a musician to take advantage of the rich and diverse music available for the entire year and to rehearse appropriate music well in advance. The recommendation to follow the liturgical year offers a freedom and versatility independent of the minister's sermon subject. James White says:

> Appropriate **hymns** are indicated in almost all denominational hymnals for seasons, festivals, and special occasions. . . . Careful use of the calendar and lectionary can be a tremendous boon to church musicians, since it gives them lead time to order and rehearse appropriate music.[2]

Of course, there may be occasions when it would be advantageous and advisable for a musician to alter or substitute a musical rendition to fit the spirit of the moment. However, this does not minimize the need for planning in advance the music of the church on a seasonal basis. The musician should also prepare a planned prelude and postlude (even if it is the improvisation of a familiar hymn tune) along with the anthem and gospel selection so that they may be announced in the Sunday bulletin.

Fifth, musicians should not assume that choir members are incapable of learning. Often musicians fail to lift the level of choir capability by assuming that members of the choir cannot learn to read music or sing anthems or improvise a hymn. Conversely, many musicians expect a high standard beyond the ability of the choir. To try to teach music that is far too difficult simply frustrates the musician as well as the choir members. Music that has a built-in possibility of failure should not be pushed upon the choir because the resulting frustration can hurt the choir's self-image. The musician must be able to assess the strengths and weaknesses, the abilities and limitations of each choir.

Sixth, musicians, through consultation with the pastor, must insist upon the enforcement of rules of discipline if he or she is to be effective. The musician, along with the pastor, is responsible for the selection and use of music in the church. This is not the responsibility of the president of the choir or any member of the choir. Reasonable expectations should be emphasized concerning rehearsal time and frequency. The musician has the right to expect choir members to cooperate in offering the congregation, and God, the very best.

Seventh, the church musician must guard against the temptation to become an entertainer. Many musicians use the church and the choir as a background for their own performances. The church musicians who also sing are constantly subject to the temptation of being the perennial lead singer. Many musicians are more concerned about the development of their own talent than about developing the music ability of the choirs they serve.

Musicians who play the organ must be careful not to allow the organ to dominate the worship experience. The musical instrument accompanies the music of the choir and congregation; it should not dominate or drown it out. This is true for accompanying solo voices as well. The organist need not play background music for every prayer or even during the sermon, for such music is often contrived and artificial. There are even times when the instruments should be silent as the people of God make their musical offering. The organist must always keep in mind that the Spirit does not cease to be felt when the instrument stops; neither does the Spirit depend upon the beat of an organ as the source of inspiration.

Finally, the musician must be prepared to take at least

partial responsibility for the musical and spiritual growth of the choir. The importance of the concept of interrelatedness within the body of Christ lies in the fact that the choir's growth is predicated upon the growth of the musician. One of the characteristics of the church choir musician is the combined ability both to assess his or her unique abilities and situation and to expect continued professional growth.

CHAPTER SEVEN

The Choir

Before delving into some of the issues concerning the function and operation of the choir, the question needs to be raised, Why have a choir at all? Of course, the obvious answer is, "Well, someone must supply the music in the worship service." A counterresponse would be, "Then, why must the choir supply the music? Why not the entire congregation?" On a deeper level, these questions would lead us to a larger query: At what point can a choir become a hindrance rather than a help in the sacred art of worship?

The Bible does not offer much direction to help us with these questions. A passage in the Old Testament (2 Chronicles 5:13-14) describes the singing of the Levitical choir. The New Testament offers no account of the existence or function of a choir even though scattered references are made concerning the use of music in the worship of the early church.

Throughout the history of the Chrisitan church, the function of the choir has been shaped by the historical context and the cultural background of a particular ecclesiastical tradition. Even the location of the choir stand or gallery has mirrored the theology of the people who worship and define the choir's function. In some religious traditions, the choir is located in a gallery area, almost hidden from the congregation's view. In other church traditions, the choir is located in a divided chancel area, an extension of the priestly function. In still other traditions, the choir is behind the central pulpit, addressing the congregation.

In the black tradition, the choir is usually located behind or at each side of the central pulpit. Some black churches, influenced by white architectural designs, have divided chancels, but these are exceptions. In the mainstream churches, the preaching of the Word is central, and the pulpit is usually located in the center of the chancel area. Of course, this does not always apply to black congregations that have purchased church buildings previously owned by white congregations and have usually left the existing architectural design intact.

Wendell Whalum, in a lecture series at Hampton Institute several years ago, suggests that the function of the choir is threefold: to speak to God *for* the congregation (responses); to speak to God *with* the congregation (hymns); and to speak *to* the congregation (special music). More shall be said later concerning this definition of the function of the choir.

Choir Status: Its Origin and Problems

The choir in the black church has an interesting history. As black churches began to emerge after the Civil War, church choirs were organized. However, this development was not without conflict. These choirs represented a wide spectrum of music, from choirs steeped in the tradition of the Fisk Jubilee Singers to note-singing (using do-re-mi) choirs and quartets in the deep South. It is essential to understand that among the black masses particularly, the black church became the center of community activity. Music became an important function and the church became, among other things, a kind of entertainment center. To some extent, the congregation became the audience, the pulpit a stage, and the folk preacher and choir the entertainers.

This development should not be looked upon disparagingly, for this type of church-centered activity filled a legitimate need of the black community as it sought meaning and relevance in the years following emancipation. In many instances singing in the choir became an escape from the pressures of the outside world. The point to remember is that the choirs in the black churches of the masses took on a prestigious quality. The choir became a status organization within the church.

(Two possible indications of status are visits to other churches and choir robes. Church choirs not only furnish music in their own churches but also visit other churches on Sunday afternoons, giving concerts and participating in choir anniversaries and festivals. Black church choirs wear robes [a development in recent decades], another symbol of social as well as religious identity. These robes are sometimes initialed and colorful.)

As the black community turned inward to find meaning in its own institutions, there emerged within the black church some of the same sociological characteristics already existing in the outside world. Because the masses of black people were ill equipped to compete in the larger society, competition developed within the black church and particularly within choirs. Today, most black churches have several choirs. In the average black church, one might find one or more of the following choirs: senior choir, gospel or inspirational choir, male chorus, young adult choir, youth (junior) choir, and children's (cherub) choir. In the past, and even today, some adult choirs are labeled choir #1, choir #2, and so on. Contemporary names for choirs include: sanctuary choir, chancel choir, ensemble, and mass choir. Many choirs bear the name of a living or deceased pastor or outstanding church member.

As a result of this elaborate choir structure within the

church, there is a tendency toward competitiveness: choirs vie for popularity and prestige. Each choir, adorned in its own color and style of robe, may even boast of having its own organist and its own particular Sunday to sing. Many choir members are more faithful to their choir than they are to the total ministry of the church.

The internal functioning of a choir may also manifest trivial and parochial concerns. Choir members who have just emerged from a war of words and ill feelings can not be instantly transformed into a "choir of angels." A choir that is unable effectively to negotiate inner conflict and differences will also have difficulty singing *for*, *with*, or *to* the congregation. Often, bitter feelings can result from the inability of choir members to decide on the color of a robe or the format of an anniversary program or the acceptance of an invitation to sing elsewhere. This is an indication of a choir's inability to come to terms with its own purpose and reason for existence.

Floyd Massey and Samuel McKinney underscore the nature of the choir situation in the black church:

> The Music Department has been called the war department of the church simply because there is more potential for conflict among groups that meet often than among those that don't. Frequency of interaction often makes groups organized to engender creative tension repositories of degenerative tension.[1]

A Choir's Threefold Function

This brings the matter again to the question, Why have a choir? How does a choir define its own *raison d'etre*? The answer to these questions depends upon whether or not the choir sees itself manufacturing a product or engaged in the offering of itself to God in the collective act of worship and praise.

Robert Mitchell brings this issue to focus. He notes:

> The music brought into Sunday's worship service will be

the public sharing of that which is happening both musically and in areas of Christian growth within the choir.

Giving priority to the process does not mean abandoning the desire for musical excellence. If the process is a good one, it will lead inevitably to the creation of good music. The achievement of this, in such a case, will not be at the expense of persons who are being exploited for what they can provide. Rather, it will come as the result of an emerging, disciplined, redemptive community that is living out and modeling the meaning of being "Christian."[2]

Now, it is important to return to the threefold function of the choir, that is to speak to God *for* the congregation, to speak *with* the congregation, and to speak *to* the congregation.

To speak to God *for* the congregation implies that the choir, as a singing unit, brings into the worship service certain skills and gifts not given to the congregation. In this sense, the choir sharpens and polishes the song of the congregation. The purpose of the choir rehearsal is to sharpen and polish the choir's skills. Rehearsal is not primarily a social gathering nor a task-oriented group in the sense of merely planning programs and raising funds, even though these activities may indeed be a part of the choir's agenda.

The choir is involved in the process of spiritual growth. It is through interaction that the songs of the people of God are made perfect. When the choir sings *for* the congregation, it is offering what the congregation cannot offer. The tools of the choir members are refined through practice, discipline, commitment, and training. The vestments of the choir are modest, but uniform, for it is not individuals making the offering, but the choir itself. It is a collective voice.

It is important to note that just as true worship is a communal experience, so the functioning of the choir is a communal experience. The choir community shapes the song, much in the same manner the slave communities shaped the spirituals. The music belongs to the group, not to the individual, and the authentic songs outlive the singers. The Negro spiritual, with its communal emphasis, also reflected the social history of black people, for it was, and is, the black church that provided the corporate structure through which blacks found meaning and purpose. The corporate nature of the black experience is underscored by Edward Wimberly who suggests that

the term *corporate* means that the care of the individual is the function of the whole community, rather than the function of the pastor or any other specially designated person who possesses specialized skills.[3]

But, not only does the choir speak *for* the congregation, it also speaks *with* the congregation. It is unfortunate that in many contemporary black churches congregational participation is minimal. This is partly due to a sparse use of hymns through which the entire congregation can participate. It is also due to the popularity of contemporary gospel songs that call for special arrangements known only to the singers.

To say that the choir sings *with* the congregation is to suggest that the choir was never intended to guard the music of the church as if that music were owned exclusively by the choir. The choir is also congregation and a participant in the act of worship. The special function of the choir is not only performance but participation. In each worship service there is a need for the choir to speak *for* the congregation and *with* the congregation.

Also the choir speaks *to* the congregation. In speaking *to* the congregation, the choir addresses the worshipers with special music, rehearsed and prepared for such a purpose. This music is the special offering of the choir and should be a commentary in music as the choir reflects upon the presence of God.

Moving Toward More Effective Ministry

These observations lead to the following recommendations as choirs in the black church seek to fulfill their purpose.

First, in many church circles the question is debated whether or not choir members should be members of the church. Church policies and practices vary. Some churches allow persons who are not members of the church to sing in the choir. Other churches insist that choir members first be members of the church. Of course, various factors may influence the position taken. Some churches lack persons equipped to sing in a choir. In order to fill the void, they have an open policy. Many churches value a high quality of music and, consequently, seek competent singers from outside their own walls.

For the health and well-being of the total church, it may be advisable to limit membership in the choir to those persons who are members of the church. The church is a whole made up of parts, and because of the interdependent nature of the body of Christ, to limit choir membership to church members may reduce potential friction from those who may not be as sensitive to the purposes and goals of the church and its ministry.

Of course, the way to avoid this possibility and still allow persons from the outside membership in the choir is to limit their participation in the decision-making processes within the group. Also it may be beneficial to allow outside participation for concerts or when special or seasonal music is offered.

Second, one of the ways to improve the quality of music in the church is to reduce the number of choirs. Most churches have too many choirs, many of which are unnecessary. It is a myth that a church needs a different choir for each Sunday in the month. To encourage the formation of more choirs in a church is to invite as well as promote competition and confusion.

The competition takes the form of each choir trying to outdo the other and each comparing itself to another and none offering an acceptable gift to God. Many choirs feel that they "own" a particular song, and no other choir in that church should sing the same song. Of course, one might argue that because of the sociological value of participation in small groups the existence of many choirs can be positive. However, the issue is whether or not the quality of the church's song should be sacrificed through the quantity of choirs and whether or not the need for belonging and identity can be made within other contexts.

This fact is underscored when one truly understands the function of the choir. White says further:

> The choir is always and only a supplement to the congregation except at sacred concerts. The choir exists only to do what the congregation cannot do or to help the congregation do its singing better.[4]

The church really needs only one adult choir and a youth choir. One reason for having so many choirs is the notion that each choir needs to specialize in a certain type of music. Consequently, there is a gospel choir, singing only gospel music; a senior choir, singing perhaps some anthems, spirituals, and "old-line" gospel songs; a young adult or young people's choir, singing only contemporary gospel; and a male chorus with a quartet sound. The choirs in a church should be versatile, not confined to one type of music.

One of the unfortunate labels placed upon at least one choir in most black churches is the label "senior." Most black churches have a senior choir. Perhaps there are other names that do not imply special rank which would be more creative and constructive. What is in a name? A great deal!

Third, one of the perennial problems in many choirs is the problem of the soloist, which is in reality the problem of the choir. Again, the gift of the individual must be weighed against the needs of the choir as a whole. The soloist does not "own" a song, nor should one or two persons render all the solos. However, it is also helpful to recognize that not all choir members are soloists.

Perhaps it would be a good idea for a solo part to be taught to at least two persons so that if one is absent, the musical offering may still be made. Also it is not advisable to allow persons in the choir to compete for a solo. This may result in ill feelings and resentment. The organist/director is in a position to know whose voice fits a particular song and should be allowed to make a selection on the basis of his or her expertise.

Fourth, churches should provide money in the budget for the operation of the choir since the choir belongs to the church. It is suggested that the church, not the individual choir members, own the choir robes, for the choir robes are church property, just as the choir is church property in the sense of accountability. Choir robes should not be faddish or profane. Their colors should reflect the symbols of Christian faith. Time should be spent teaching the colors of the Christian church, and this knowledge should guide the selection of style and color of the robes. Long dresses and brightly colored suits are not proper attire to offer God in worship. The aim of the choir member is not to show self but to engage in collective worship in the presence of the holy.

Fifth, choir members must always guard against the temptation to exhibit self. There are many manifestations of excesses in the black church. One of the most disturbing is the tendency of many choirs to become exhibitionists and performers. Many soloists thrive on attention received as they parade from front door to back door. Much of this is contrived and artificial. Verses of songs are sung over and over again in an attempt to manufacture emotional responses. Excessive clapping and swaying sometimes detract from the song, and many choirs seem more concerned with form than substance. Clapping, swaying, and other forms of movement are an integral part of the black tradition and should be affirmed as legitimate worship expressions. These forms are part of the African survival.

However, they must come out of an understanding of the meaning of worship. James White notes that worship involves the whole person. He says,

> The whole body participates in worship through various **postures** . . . **gestures** . . . and **movement**. . . . Even our **clothing** is an important part of worship. It testifies to our understanding of the occasion and our role in it as well as facilitating or constraining meaningful movement.[5]

Sixth, the choirs in the black church of the masses spend much of their time and energy participating in choir anniversaries. The usual format for these annual events is for choirs from local churches to render two or more selections. These choir festivals are frequent in black churches, especially in those whose members feel a greater sense of social and economic disenfranchisement. Such events are entertaining and tend to be competitive as each choir seeks to outsing and outperform other participants. Gospel music is used almost exclusively. The real essence of worship is usually lost in such a theatrical atmosphere.

An alternative would be to bring choirs together to participate in concerts of sacred music. Music could be sent to cooperating choirs in advance. The head director could visit various choir rehearsals to make sure that the music is taught properly. The format should include a variety of music: hymns, spirituals, meter hymns, anthems, and gospel. This would reduce the competitive nature of such anniversaries and provide the context for a cultural as well as a religious experience for both participants and congregation. It would also satisfy the need for social interaction. The educational value of such an effort would be in sharpening the appreciation and understanding the variety of music historically utilized in the black religious experience.

The Youth Choir

Most churches have a junior or youth choir made up of children and adolescents. Some churches allow young people to participate in the youth choir even if they are not members of the church. This practice, if unchecked, may lead to the attitude that singing in the choir is the sum total of one's confession of faith. Consequently, children may grow into adulthood remaining only at the periphery of church life.

An alternative practice might be to allow young children some degree of participation in a children's choir with the understanding that they will be nurtured and directed toward a meaningful commitment to God and the church.

Through youth, who may be initially drawn to the church because of music, the black church has an excellent opportunity to minister to the black family. J. Deotis Roberts sees this ministry as crucial in balancing the priestly and prophetic role of the black church. The involvement of young people in the youth choir must be seen in a larger context. "Ministry to black families," says Roberts, "has to take under review the external social, political, and economic factors that relate to black family crises."[6]

There is a great deal the black church can do to improve the quality of music, beginning with its children. The church has an urgent educational task to train its youth. If the church desires a trained choir, it must train its youth. The church should not allow youth to dictate the type and style of music used. Rather, the church and its leadership should offer youth the best within the church's music tradition. The repertoire of the youth choir should move beyond contemporary gospel music, especially when most of the shallow lyrics are far removed from the child's perceptions and experiences.

Members of the youth choir should be taught the proper way to offer a hymn. Spirituals and meter hymns as well as anthems might be utilized. The church is mandated to give youth what they need, rather than to encourage the latest fads in order to keep youth interested and involved.

It has already been suggested that music appreciation classes might be incorporated in the youth activities so that children may appreciate the range and scope of the contributions of black composers and their compositions. Youth should be taught to read music. Organ and piano classes may be sponsored by the church to encourage and develop musicians of the future.

Music should be used that fits the ages of children. Music compositions may be transposed to fit children's voices. At very young ages children's voices may lend themselves more readily to unison singing rather than harmony. It is also important to recognize that a children's choir speaks to God *for, with,* and *to* the congregation in words, thoughts, and images that reflect the perceptions and experiences of a child. It is essential that one does not dismiss the music offering of the child as merely cute. If religious education is taken seriously, the church will train its young for more perfect service to God.

CHAPTER EIGHT

Conclusions

The purpose of this book is to raise contemporary issues concerning the music of the black church. In order to accomplish this task it was necessary to anchor the study in the Judeo-Christian witness of the Bible, which is the record of divine-human encounter. The aim has been to make the contemporary black minister more aware of these issues and to take a closer look at the pastor-musician-choir-congregation relationship. Since music is such an important component in the worship experience, it is essential that black Americans concern themselves with a continuing effort to measure their present situation against a biblical understanding of the purpose and function of music in worship. It has been noted that in both Old and New Testaments, the central aim of worship as well as of the music used in worship, is the edification of the family of God.

I have sought to identify some of the characteristics of Afro-American culture and the music of black people born out of despair but punctuated with hope. It is essential that each generation evaluate its past and critically analyze its present so that it may correct the course along the religious pilgrimage. Music may be used either to glorify God or to manipulate authentic human experience.

I have suggested the need for a greater degree of pastoral leadership in dealing with the issues presented as pastor, musician, choir, and congregation form a partnership to improve the quality of the worship experience through the use of the music of the people of God. The task is an educational one, beginning with youth. The task is a corporate one, for we witness and worship in the context of others who share their faith in a living God, who deserves and demands their best.

It is to this end that these guidelines to improve the quality of music in the black church have been offered.

Notes

Chapter 1

[1] Henry Mitchell, *Black Preaching* (New York: J. B. Lippincott Co., 1970), pp. 43-47.

[2] Eileen Southern, *The Music of Black Americans* (New York: W. W. Norton & Co., Inc., 1971), p. 14.

[3] *Ibid.*, p. 16.

[4] Dena J. Epstein, *Sinful Tunes and Spirituals* (Champaign, Ill.: University of Illinois Press, 1977), p. 343.

[5] Wyatt Tee Walker, *Somebody's Calling My Name* (Valley Forge: Judson Press, 1979), p. 29.

[6] Southern, *Music of Black Americans*, p. 18.

[7] Miles Mark Fisher, *Negro Slave Songs in the United States* (New York: Citadel Press, 1953), pp. 25-26.

[8] Mitchell, *Black Preaching*, p. 167.

[9] J. Deotis Roberts, *Roots of a Black Future: Family and Church* (Philadelphia: The Westminster Press, 1980), pp. 114-115.

[10] James H. Cone, *The Spirituals and the Blues: An Interpretation* (New York: The Seabury Press, Inc., 1972), p. 5.

Chapter 2

[1] Oscar Cullmann, *Early Christian Worship*, trans. A. Stewart Todd and James B. Torrance (Philadelphia: The Westminster Press, 1953), p. 11.

[2] Ferdinand Hahn, *The Worship of the Early Church*, ed. John Reumann, trans. David E. Green (Philadelphia: Fortress Press, 1973), pp. 105-108.

[3] Ralph P. Martin, *Worship in the Early Church* (Old Tappan, N.J.: Fleming H. Revell, 1964), p. 48.

[4]Gerhard Delling, *Worship in the New Testament*, trans. P. Scott (Philadelphia: Fortress Press, 1973), p. 86.

[5]Eric Routley, *Music Leadership in the Church* (Nashville: Abingdon Press, 1967), p. 88.

Chapter 3

[1]Henry Mitchell, "Black Preaching," *Review and Expositor* (Summer, 1973), p. 334.

[2]Wyatt Tee Walker, *Somebody's Calling My Name* (Valley Forge: Judson Press, 1979), pp. 52-58.

[3]Wendell Whalum, "Black Hymnody," *Review and Expositor* (1973), vol. 70, pp. 347-349.

[4]Walker, *Somebody's Calling My Name*, p. 144.

[5]Olin P. Moyd, *Redemption in Black Theology* (Valley Forge: Judson Press, 1979), p. 23.

Chapter 4

[1]J. Deotis Roberts, "The Black Caucus and the Failure of Christian Theology," *The Journal of Religious Thought* (1969), vol. 26, p. 15.

[2]J. Deotis Roberts, *Roots of a Black Future: Family and Church* (Philadelphia: The Westminster Press, 1980), p. 115.

[3]Willi Apel, *Harvard Dictionary of Music* (Cambridge, Mass.: Harvard University Press, Belknap Press, 1944 and 1969), p. 397.

[4]Austin C. Lovelace, *The Organist and Hymn Playing* (Nashville: Abingdon Press, 1962), p. 28.

[5]Jack C. Goode, *Pipe Organ Registration* (Nashville: Abingdon Press, 1964), p. 163.

[6]James F. White, *Introduction to Christian Worship* (Nashville: Abingdon Press, 1980), p. 246.

[7]*Ibid.*, p. 249.

[8]Andrew Watterson Blackwood, *The Funeral* (Philadelphia: The Westminster Press, 1942), p. 64.

[9]White, *Introduction to Christian Worship*, p. 268.

[10]*Ibid.*, p. 269.

[11]Paul E. Irion, *The Funeral and the Mourners* (Nashville: Abingdon Press, 1954), p. 77.

[12]Edward P. Wimberly, *Pastoral Care in the Black Church* (Nashville: Abingdon Press, 1979), pp. 91-92.

Chapter 5

[1]James Earl Massey, *The Responsible Pulpit* (Anderson, Ind.: Warner Press, 1974), p. 42.

[2]*Ibid.*, pp. 42-43.

[3] Robert H. Mitchell, *Ministry and Music* (Philadelphia: The Westminster Press, 1978), p. 62.

[4] For further information about this view of the church, see Alvin J. Lindgren and Norman Shawchuck, *Management for Your Church* (Nashville: Abingdon Press, 1977).

[5] Mitchell, *Ministry and Music*, p. 60.

Chapter 6

[1] Gustave Reese, *Music in the Renaissance* (New York: W. W. Norton & Co., Inc., 1959), pp. 711-712.

[2] James F. White, *Introduction to Christian Worship* (Nashville: Abingdon Press, 1980), p. 72.

Chapter 7

[1] Floyd Massey, Jr., and Samuel Berry McKinney, *Church Administration in the Black Perspective* (Valley Forge: Judson Press, 1976), p. 42.

[2] Robert H. Mitchell, *Ministry and Music* (Philadelphia: The Westminster Press, 1978), p. 58.

[3] Edward P. Wimberly, *Pastoral Counseling and Spiritual Values* (Nashville: Abingdon Press, 1982), p. 26.

[4] James F. White, *Introduction to Christian Worship* (Nashville: Abindgon Press, 1980), p. 102.

[5] *Ibid.*, p. 103.

[6] J. Deotis Roberts, *Roots of a Black Future: Family and Church* (Philadelphia: The Westminster Press, 1980), p. 119.

Bibliography

Abba, Raymond, *Principles of Christian Worship*. New York: Oxford University Press, Inc., 1957.

von Allmen, Jean Jacques, *Worship: Its Theology and Practice*. New York: Oxford University Press, Inc., 1965.

Anderson, James D., and Jones, Ezra E., *The Management of Ministry*. New York: Harper & Row, Publishers, Inc., 1978.

Apel, Willi, *Harvard Dictionary of Music*. Cambridge, Mass.: Harvard University Press, 1944.

Berger, Peter L., *The Noise of Solemn Assemblies*. New York: Doubleday & Co., Inc., 1961.

Biersdorf, John E., ed., *Creating an Intentional Ministry*. Nashville: Abingdon Press, 1976.

Blackwood, Andrew W., *The Fine Art of Public Worship*. Nashville: Abingdon Press, 1939.

Blackwood, Andrew W., *The Funeral*. Philadelphia: The Westminster Press, 1942.

Cone, James H., *The Spirituals and the Blues*. New York: The Seabury Press, Inc., 1972.

Cronbach, Abraham, "Jewish Worship in New Testament Times," *The Interpreter's Dictionary of the Bible* (Vol. 4), edited by George Arthur Buttrick. Nashville: Abingdon Press, 1962.

Cullmann, Oscar, *Early Christian Worship*. Trans. A. Stewart Todd and James B. Torrance. Philadelphia: The Westminster Press, 1953.

Cuney-Hare, Maud, *Negro Musicians and Their Music*. Washington: The Associated Publishers, Inc., 1936.

Davies, J. G., ed., *A Dictionary of Liturgy and Worship*. New York: Macmillan Inc., 1972.

Davison, Archibald, *Protestant Church Music in America*. Boston: Schirmer Books, 1933.

DeLerma, Dominique-Rene, *Black Music in Our Culture*. Kent, Ohio: Kent State University Press, 1970.

Delling, Gerhard, *Worship in the New Testament*. Trans. P. Scott. Philadelphia: Fortress Press, 1973.

Douglass, Winfred, *Church Music in History and Practice*. New York: Charles Scribner's, Sons, 1937.

DuBois, W. E. B., *The Gift of Black Folk*. New York: Johnson Books, 1968.

Epstein, Dena J., *Sinful Tunes and Spirituals: Black Folk Music to the Civil War*. Champaign, Ill.: University of Illinois Press, 1981.

Ewen, D., *Hebrew Music*. New York: Bloch Publishing Co., Inc., 1931.

Fisher, Miles M., *Negro Slave Songs in the United States*. New York: Citadel Press, 1953.

Frazier, E. Franklin, *The Negro Church in America*. New York: Schocken Books, Inc., 1973.

Frazier, E. Franklin, and Lincoln, C. Eric, *The Black Church Since Frazier*. New York: Schocken Books, Inc., 1974.

Goode, Jack C., *Pipe Organ Registration*. Nashville: Abingdon Press, 1964.

Hahn, Ferdinand, *The Worship of the Early Church*. Ed. John Reumann, trans. David E. Green. Philadelphia: Fortress Press, 1973.

Halter, Carl, *The Practice of Sacred Music*. St. Louis: Concordia Publishing House, 1955.

Heilbut, Tony, *The Gospel Sound*. New York: Simon and Schuster, 1971.

Herskovitz, M. J., *The Myth of the Negro Past*. Boston: Beacon Press, 1958.

Hoon, Paul W., *The Integrity of Worship*. Nashville: Abingdon Press, 1968.

Hunter, Archibald M., *Paul and His Predecessors*. Philadelphia: The Westminster Press, 1961.

Irion, Paul E., *The Funeral and the Mourners*. Nashville: Abingdon Press, 1954.

Jones, Ilion, *A Historical Approach to Evangelical Worship*. Nashville: Abingdon Press, 1954.

Kirkpatrick, Alexander F., *The Book of Psalms*. Cambridge: Cambridge University Press, 1902.

Kummel, W., *The Theology of the New Testament*. Trans. John E. Steely. Nashville: Abingdon Press, 1973.

Levine, Lawrence J., *Black Culture and Black Consciousness: Afro-American Folk Thought from Slavery to Freedom*. New York: Oxford University Press, 1977.

Lincoln, C. Eric, ed., *The Black Experience in Religion*. New York: Anchor Press, 1974.

Lindgren, A., and Shawchuck, N., *Management for Your Church: How to Realize Your Church's Potential Through a Systems Approach*. Nashville: Abingdon Press, 1977.

Lovelace, Austin C., *The Organist and Hymn Playing*. Nashville: Abingdon Press, 1962.

Lovell, John, Jr., *Black Song: The Forge and the Flame*. New York: Macmillan Inc., 1972.

Lowth, R., *Lectures on the sacred poetry of the Hebrews*. London: S. Chadwick & Co., 1847.

Macleod, D., "Theology Gives Meaning and Shape to Worship." *The Princeton Seminary Bulletin*, 1975, pp. 37-47.

Martin, Ralph P., *Worship in the Early Church*. Old Tappan, N.J.: Fleming H. Revell, 1964.

Massey, James E., *The Responsible Pulpit*. Anderson, Ind.: Warner Press Inc., 1974.

Massey, Floyd, Jr., and McKinney, Samuel Berry, *Church Administration in the Black Perspective*. Valley Forge: Judson Press, 1976.

Maxwell, William D., *An Outline of Christian Worship*. New York: Oxford University Press, 1936.

Mays, B., *The Negro's God*. Boston: Chapman and Grimes, Inc., 1938.

Moule, C. F. D., *Worship in the New Testament*. Atlanta: John Knox Press, 1961.

Mitchell, Henry, *Black Preaching*. New York: Harper & Row Publishing, Inc., 1979.

Mitchell, Robert H., *Ministry and Music*. Philadelphia: The Westminster Press, 1978.

Moyd, Olin P., *Redemption in Black Theology*. Valley Forge: Judson Press, 1979.

Pierik, Marie, *The Psalter in the Temple and the Church*. Washington: Catholic University of America Press, 1957.

Reese, Gustave, *Music in the Renaissance*. New York: W. W. Norton & Co., Inc., 1954.

Richardson, C. C., "Christian Worship in New Testament Times," *The Interpreter's Dictionary of the Bible* (Vol. 4), edited by George Arthur Buttrick. Nashville: Abingdon Press, 1962.

Ricks, George R., *Some Aspects of the Religious Music of the United States Negro*. Ed. Richard M. Dorson. New York: Arno Press, Inc., 1960.

Ringgren, Helmer, *Israelite Religion*. Trans. David E. Green. Philadelphia: Fortress Press, 1966.

Roberts, J. Deotis, "The Black Caucus and the Failures of Christian Theology." *The Journal of Religious Thought*, 1969, vol. 26, p. 15.

Roberts, J. Deotis, *Roots of a Black Future: Family and Church*. Philadelphia: The Westminster Press, 1980.

Routley, Erik, *The Church and Music*. London: Duckworth & Co., Ltd., 1950.

Routley, Erik, *The Organist's Guide to Congregational Praise*.

London: Independent Press, Ltd., 1957.

Routley, Erik, *Church Music and Theology*. Philadelphia: Fortress Press, 1959.

Routley, Erik, *Words, Music, and Theology*. Nashville: Abingdon Press, 1968.

Routley, Erik, and Young, Carlton R., *Music Leadership in the Church*. Nashville: Abingdon, 1967.

Rylaarsdam, J. Coert, *Revelation in Jewish Wisdom Literature*. Chicago: University of Chicago Press, 1946.

Schalk, C., "Thoughts on Smashing Idols: Church Music in the '80s." *The Christian Century*, 1980, vol. 98, pp. 960-963.

Scott, Ernest F., "The Beginnings." *The Interpreter's Bible* (Vol. 7), edited by George Arthur Buttrick. Nashville: Abingdon Press, 1951.

Segler, Franklin, *Christian Worship: Its Theology and Practice*. Nashville: Broadman Press, 1963.

Shepherd, Massey H., Jr., ed., *Worship in Scripture and Tradition*. New York: Oxford University Press, Inc., 1963.

Skoglund, John E., *Worship in the Free Churches*. Valley Forge: Judson Press, 1965.

Southern, Eileen, *The Music of Black Americans: A History*. New York: W. W. Norton & Co., Inc., 1971.

Stookey, L., "Thinking Theologically About Worship." Mimeographed, privately distributed.

Sydnor, James R., *The Training of Church Choirs*. Nashville: Abingdon Press, 1963.

Thomas, Latta R., *Biblical Faith and the Black American*. Valley Forge: Judson Press, 1976.

Underhill, Evelyn, *Worship*. New York: Harper & Row Publishers, Inc., 1957. (Originally published 1937.)

Walker, Wyatt Tee, *Somebody's Calling My Name*. Valley Forge: Judson Press, 1979.

Whalum, Wendell, "Black Hymnody." *Review & Expositor*, 1973, vol. 70, pp. 341-355.

Whalum, Wendell, "Church Music: A Position Paper (with special consideration of music in the black church)."

Privately distributed, 1975, but available from Morehouse College, Box 703, Atlanta, Georgia 30314.

White, James F., *Introduction to Christian Worship*. Nashville: Abingdon Press, 1981.

Wilmore, Gayraud S., *Black Religion and Black Radicalism: An Interpretation of the Religious History of Afro-American People*. New York: Doubleday & Co., Inc., 1972.

Wilson, John, *Introduction to Church Music*. Chicago: Moody Press, 1965.

Wimberly, Edward P., *Pastoral Counseling and Spiritual Values: A Black Point of View*. Nashville: Abingdon Press, 1982.

Work, J., "Plantation Meistersinger." *The Musical Quarterly*, 1941, vol. 27, pp. 97-106.